Dictionary of Advertising and Marketing Concepts

Dictionary of
Advertising and
Marketing Concepts

Arthur Asa Berger

Left
Coast
Press
Inc.

Walnut Creek, California

LEFT COAST PRESS, INC.
1630 North Main Street, #400
Walnut Creek, CA 94596
http://www.LCoastPress.com

ISBN 978-1-61132-985-8 hardcover
ISBN 978-1-61132-986-5 paperback
ISBN 978-1-61132-987-2 institutional eBook
ISBN 978-1-61132-752-6 consumer eBook

Library of Congress Cataloging-in-Publication Data:

Berger, Arthur Asa, 1933-
  Dictionary of advertising and marketing concepts / Arthur Asa Berger.
     pages cm
  Summary: "From AdBusters to viral marketing, this brief dictionary of ideas and concepts contains over 100 extended, illuminating entries to bring the novice up to speed on the advertising/marketing world and the ideas that underlie it. For the neophyte professional, it describes the various players and strategies of the industry. For the student, it summarizes the key ideas of the most important cultural theorists introduced in advertising and marketing courses. For everyone, it helps explain the cultural, economic, and psychological role that advertising concepts play in society. A handy introduction for students and a quick reference for young professionals"—Provided by publisher.
  Includes bibliographical references.
  ISBN 978-1-61132-985-8 (hardback)—ISBN 978-1-61132-986-5 (paperback)—ISBN 978-1-61132-987-2 (institutional ebook)—ISBN 978-1-61132-752-6 (consumer eBook)

  1. Advertising—Dictionaries. 2. Marketing—Dictionaries. I. Title.
  HF5803.B47 2013
  658.8003—dc23
                    2013024530

Printed in the United States of America

⊗™ The paper used in this publication meets the minimum requirements of American National Standard for Information Sciences—Permanence of Paper for Printed Library Materials, ANSI/NISO Z39.48–1992.

I am reminded all too often as to just how chuckleheaded and indolent many people in the ad business can be. Over the years, I collected a file filled with hundreds and hundreds of ads for hundreds and hundreds of advertisers and brands. The file included ads for handbags, watches, liquors, wines, airlines, destinations, jewelry, lingerie, shoes, perfumes, candy, eyeglasses, shirts, automobiles, and on and on. Every one of these ads had a different visual from all others, and most had a photo of the product itself. That alone would be cause for concern because simply showing the product is not often enough motivation to change a perception, much less convince someone to buy.

But the remarkable thing is that every one of these ads had essentially the same headline. They all began with the same three words: The Art of.... followed by one other.

The Art of Living
The Art of Flying
The Art of Dressing
The Art of Wine
The Art of Design
The Art of Engineering
The Art of BS

Not only does this dearth of creativity fail in attention getting and motivation, it also diminishes the credibility of the claims and the image of the brand. If so many other brands are saying they are "The Art of...," what does that say about my brand? Not much.

The prevalence of using this headline in so many ads demonstrates an incredible lack of respect for the perception and intelligence of the consumers who are, of course, exposed to all these identical claims for so many products.

Another solution that far too many creative people chance upon is the use of a celebrity. It has been said, "When you have nothing to say, get a celebrity." And sometimes this works if there is a perfect fit between the product and the person. But it also requires a great creative link expressed in the advertisement.

I was involved once with a commercial for an analgesic where the client insisted on using a celebrity as spokesperson despite being shown many more clever, relevant, and persuasive ideas. The client prevailed, and at great cost the celebrity was secured, commercials were shot and then aired on national TV. Everybody remembered the commercials and John Wayne: nobody remembered what the product was that he was talking about.

Arguably the single most important reason for the existence of so much less than effective, truly bad, and offensive (that is, dumb) advertising is that the people responsible for developing the ads and the ones responsible for approving them haven't a clue what a great, or even good ad looks like. They judge predominantly on how strategic it is or whether it is legal or not, and often use even less relevant criteria like "that's not the way we did the last one." A great ad is one that causes someone to react viscerally and emotionally to a piece of creative work, a concept set before his or her eyes, and to say: Yes! That's it! That's great! Let's do it!

Happily, I have had the good fortune to see this kind of reaction many times over the course of my life in advertising, and it is a wonderful thing indeed. Even more wonderful are the results from utilizing this level of advertising. Unfortunately, for many in the ad game these occasions are few and far between. Quoting from my book, *The Insanity of Advertising,* "The only thing harder than creating a great ad is selling it." Oh, how true this is.

Regardless of whether you know a good ad from a bad one, if you're contemplating advertising or marketing as a career, want to learn more about it and some of its intricacies, or are simply just generally interested in what the business is about, Arthur Berger's *Dictionary of Advertising and Marketing Concepts* provides an insightful and expedient way to get an immediate global grasp of it all. Well, a lot of it.

You won't learn everything, but you'll discover enough to carry on an intelligent conversation at your next cocktail party as to what they really said and meant on last week's *Mad Men* episode.

> Fred S. Goldberg
> Ex Ad Man/Ex Mad Man
> Former COO Chiat/Day Advertising
> Founder/Former CEO Goldberg Moser O'Neill
> Author of new book:
> > *The Insanity of Advertising (Memoirs of a Mad Man)*

Acknowledgments

Let me start by thanking Mitch "The Great Rejecter" Allen for suggesting I write this book. We had met for a dim sum lunch on Clement Street—something we've been doing twice a year for the past twenty or thirty years—and at the end of the meal Mitch and I got into a conversation about what new books I might write for him. "What about a dictionary of cultural analyses and critiques of advertising?" he asked. I liked the idea and said I'd do it. I've never written a dictionary before and found the format to be surprisingly interesting and useful.

The question I faced in doing the dictionary is the one all dictionary makers must confront: What do you put in and what do you leave out? I've put in the concepts that I think are most important for understanding the impact advertising and marketing have upon our psyches, our culture, and our society. I've also discussed a number of terms used in advertising when they have cultural relevance.

I would also like to thank Fred Goldberg, founder and former head of Goldberg Moser O'Neill (where I spent three weeks as a visiting professor, thanks to the Advertising Education Foundation), for writing a foreword to this book.

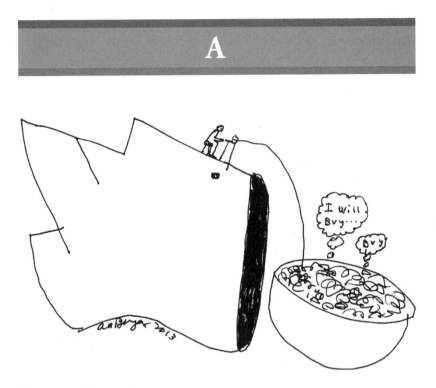

Account Executives
(also known as Account Directors and Account Managers)

Account executives mediate between the companies hiring the advertising agency and the agency and are supposed to look after the interests of both the clients and the agency. Large corporations that hire advertising agencies usually have their own advertising departments, responsible for selecting advertising agencies, and one of the most important tasks of account executives is to do what they can to satisfy the executives in the corporate advertising divisions. Some cynics in the industry, generally on the creative side of agencies, suggest that what account executives (whatever their title) do best is take people to lunch.

Dictionary of Advertising ad Marketing Concepts by Arthur Asa Berger, 11–141.

Acronym

Acronyms are words that are formed from the initial letters of a name or a series of words. Acronyms are useful in advertising because they provide an easy way for people to remember things like the names of products. One of the most well-known is UNESCO which stands for the United Nations Educational, Scientific and Cultural Organization. UNESCO World Heritage tourism sites make prominent use of this designation and the UNESCO logo in their advertising.

Adbusters (Culturejammers)

This is the name for a movement of people who attack advertising for fostering materialism and generating consumer culture. They also publish *Adbusters,* an anti-consumerist magazine: www.adbusters.org.

Advertising

The word advertising means, literally, "to turn attention to" or "to turn toward" ("ad" means "toward" and "vertire" means "to turn"). This definition suggests that advertising continually seeks to attract attention and, after doing so, to stimulate desire that will lead to action which, it is hoped, eventuates in the purchase of a product or service. Advertising plays an important role in all modern societies and, according to some critics, not only shapes our cultures and societies but also affects—as a result of the success of fast food advertising and medical advertising—our bodies and our health. Advertising, as people in the industry sometimes put it, "tells people what they want before they know they want it."

In *The Mechanical Bride* (1967, Boston: Beacon Press), Marshall McLuhan has some interesting things to say about advertising and how the advertising industry is similar to Hollywood. He writes (p. 97):

> Hollywood is like the ad agencies in constantly striving to enter and control the unconscious minds of a vast public, not in order

This is one of a series of beautifully photographed and sexually arousing advertisements from Cabana Cachaca, a Brazilian liquor company that has been criticized by some media theorists for exploiting the female body for its own purposes. Notice how the part of the woman's body that is not tanned leads our eyes towards her vagina and note, also, the phallic nature of the bottle.

to understand or to present these minds, as a serious novelist does, but in order to exploit them for profit....The ad agencies and Hollywood, in their different ways, are always trying to get inside the public mind in order to impose their collective dreams on that inner stage. And in pursuit of this goal both Hollywood and the advertising agencies give major exhibitions of unconscious behavior....The ad agencies flood the daytime world of conscious purpose and control with erotic imagery from the night world in order to drown, by suggestion, all sales resistance.

McLuhan is interested in advertising because, like Hollywood, advertising reveals the passions that shape people's behavior. He devoted his book to reprinting and analyzing a number of advertisements in terms of what they teach us about the collective psyche in the United States. I relate other comments he made about the industry in my discussion of advertising agencies.

In his foreword to my book, *Ads, Fads and Consumer Culture* (2011 Lanham, MD: Rowman & Littlefield), Fred S. Goldberg, who worked in advertising for thirty-four years and was the president of Goldberg Moser O'Neill, explains the negative effects on advertising caused by the clients of the agencies and infighting by some executives in advertising agencies:

> When you study advertising and advertising's impact, it helps to understand the context within which advertising messages are developed, produced and aired. Many of the print ads and commercials that consumers ultimately see could have been demonstrably different, were it not for the conflicting interests that went hand in hand with their development.
>
> In theory, advertisers hire agencies to create ads that will break through and impact their customers and potential customers. They hope to maximize the effectiveness of often limited media and promotional dollars, achieve a competitive edge, and gain extra mileage from each advertising message.
>
> Yet, because of the nature of the industry and the agency and client relationship, a series of conflicts often prevents this from happening as frequently as it should.
>
> And this explains, at least in part, why there is so much advertising that is spurious, curious, muddled and jumbled.... These conflicts have a numbing consequence on the impact of the clients; advertising dollars and the subsequent success they have in the marketplace selling their products or positioning their companies or causes. The advertising business is unique and particularly difficult because it is fraught with these conflicts which often result in a dumbed-down final product. (p. xi)

Goldberg calls our attention to the complications involved in creating advertising. There are often conflicts in advertising agencies between their account management representatives, who are trying to support the views of the client, and the copywriters, art directors, and creative directors in the agency, who have different opinions about how best to advertise a product. In addition, the taste of the clients often affects things. Too often, what we get in an advertisement or commercial is an unhappy compromise. I spent three weeks as a visiting professor, sponsored by the Advertising Education Foundation, at Goldberg Moser O'Neill, and Fred Goldberg told me that an agency often produces a brilliant commercial which is killed because the president of the corporation brings it home, shows it to his wife, and she doesn't like it. If you watch *Mad Men* you can get an idea of the conflicts that can occur in an advertising agency.

If we watch commercial television for four hours a day, which is the national average in the United States now, we are exposed to more than an hour of commercials each day, to which we must add the advertisements we see on the internet and on cell phones, in newspapers and magazines, and on billboards. Some researchers suggest we are exposed to as many as three thousand advertising messages each day. Marshall McLuhan has suggested that we get more pleasure from the ads for products than from the products, which suggests that advertising plays a much larger role in our lives than we might imagine, in part because advertising is so ubiquitous in American society.

Statistics about the advertising industry are difficult to obtain and often unreliable. Yet there are statistics that give us some data about the size of the industry, which offers us insights into its power. According to Plunkett Research Limited, the global advertising industry is a 449 billion dollar industry and the advertising industry in the United States is around a 173 billion dollar industry. There are approximately 6.6 billion people in the world and 300 million people in the United States.

World	United States
6.6 billion people	300 million people
$449 billion	$173 billion

What this table shows is that Americans are subjected to much more advertising than people in other countries. We have approximately one twentieth of the world's population but we spend more than one third of the amount of money spent globally for advertising.

In recent years the amount of money spent on purchasing products on the internet has grown enormously, and now, with the development of social media sites such as Facebook, Pinterest, and Twitter, advertising agencies are increasingly turning their attention to advertising on the internet. When there is an audience of more than a billion people using Facebook, advertisers find using social media and other internet sites for their purposes not only tempting but irresistible. The growth of advertising on social media sites and the internet has been very rapid.

There is a great deal of interest in the United States about advertising, as reflected in the following statistics based on a search on Google and figures from Amazon.com books (accessed January 16, 2013).

Sites on Google

Advertising	1,820,000,000
Marketing	1,940,000,000
Advertising and Society	822,000,000

Books at Amazon

Advertising	55,900
Marketing	541,000

In the United States, advertising has reached its highest level of concentration, and Americans are exposed to more advertising than people in any other country. And advertising is now a major player in many areas of life in America—including politics. For example, in the 2012 campaigns for president and for congress, billions of dollars were spent on political advertising, and the amount of money spent in the United States on advertising grows with every election. In recent years, pharmaceutical companies have spent a great deal of money on advertising, and certain television programs, such as *60 Minutes,* which have many elderly viewers, are full of commercials for medicines of one kind or another—all with disclaimers about the terrible side effects that can be experienced by those taking the medicine being advertised. Many Americans know very little about history, literature, and the arts—what we might call "cultural knowledge"—but they have a great deal of what I call "product knowledge," thanks to the power and ubiquity of advertising.

Advertising Age

Advertising Age is the most important trade journal of the advertising industry in the United States. It is possible to read some material at no charge on the internet from *Advertising Age,* which deals with news, issues of concern to advertisers, and other topics of interest relating to the advertising industry. You can access it at www.adage.com.

Advertising Agencies

Advertising agencies are media businesses that create print advertisements, radio and television commercials, and advertisements for the internet and various websites, especially social media ones. The major agencies are structured like other large businesses with chief executive officers, chief financial officers, chief marketing officers and all kinds of other specialists of one kind or another. Conventionally, agencies have two main divisions: one housing the creative directors, copywriters, artists, designers, and others directly involved in the creation of advertisements, and the other housing the administrators, account executives, media buyers, ad infinitum. In some agencies, many of the people who work in them have an impact on the creation of the advertising, though it is the creative directors and their teams of copywriters and artists who actually make the advertisements and commercials. There are often conflicts among different groups in advertising agencies which affect, generally in negative ways, the quality of the advertisements and commercials.

In *Advertising: Principles and Practice* (7th edition, 2005, Upper Saddle River, NJ: Pearson/Prentice Hall), by William Wells, Sandra Moriarty, and John Burnett, we find the following items in their description of how large, full-service agencies are organized:

Account Management
Creative Development and Production
Media Planning and Buying
Account Planning and Research
Internal Agency Services

These areas all have different tasks and responsibilities. In recent years, gigantic advertising conglomerates, made up of agencies all over the world, have developed to service the global needs of some of their clients.

Advertorials

"Advertorials" are combinations of advertisements and editorials. They look like editorials but are really advertisements. Advertorials work by tricking readers or viewers into thinking they are editorials and thus evading the negative feelings many people have about being exposed to advertisements and the lack of trust they have in the truthfulness of advertisements. There is an ethical problem involved with advertorials because they are tricking people into thinking they are reading editorials and thus are, many critics would say, immoral.

Advertising Educational Foundation (AEF)

This foundation deals with advertising and its relation to society. As it states on its website, www.aef.com:

AEF provides educational content to enrich the understanding of advertising and its role in culture, society and the economy.

MAJOR PROJECTS
• Submit paper for the Alfred J. Seaman Student Award
• Advertising & Society Review
• ADText: Advertising Curriculum

The foundation publishes a journal on advertising and also makes it possible for scholars interested in advertising to spend time at advertising agencies.

Adweek

Adweek is, as its name suggests, a weekly magazine that deals with the advertising industry. It is possible to get free emails daily from the magazine by going to www.adweek.com. There are a variety of digital newsletters and other publications available there.

Alienation

The term "alienation" means no ties or connections with others. ("A" means "no" and "lien" means "ties" or "connections.") Marxist media theorists argue that alienation is an essential feature of capitalism, which can produce goods in great quantities but also generates alienation among everyone—rich and poor, members of both the proletariat and the ruling classes. Alienation is functional for capitalism, Marxist theorists suggest, because people become obsessed with consumption as a means of temporarily escaping from painful feelings of alienation they experience.

Marx explained his views about alienation as follows:

In what does this alienation of labour consist? First, that the work is *external* to the worker, that it is not a part of his nature, that consequently he does not fulfill himself in his work but denies himself, has a feeling of misery, not of wellbeing, does not develop freely a physical and mental energy, but is physically exhausted and mentally debased. The worker therefore feels himself at home only during his leisure, whereas at work he feels homeless. His work is not voluntary but imposed, *forced labour.* It is not the satisfaction of a need, but only a *means* for satisfying other needs. Its alien character is clearly shown by the fact that as soon as there is no physical or other compulsion it is avoided like the plague. Finally, the alienated character of work for the worker appears in the fact that it is not his work but work for someone else, that in work he does not belong to himself but to another person. (In T. B. Bottomore and M. Rubel, Eds., 1964, *Selected Writings in Sociology and Social Philosophy,* New York: McGraw-Hill, pp. 169–170)

According to Marx, then, when we are alienated we become separated from our work, our friends, and from ourselves. Our work, which is central to our identity and our sense of self, becomes separated from us and ends up as a destructive force. We experience ourselves as objects, as things that are acted upon by others, and not as subjects or active forces. And what we produce becomes "commodities," objects separated from our labor. As we become increasingly more alienated, we become the prisoners of our alienated needs and end up, as Marx puts it, as *"self-conscious* and *self-acting"* commodities (quoted in E. Fromm, 1962, *Beyond the Chains of Illusion: My Encounter with Marx and Freud,* New York: Simon and Schuster, p. 51).

Marx believed that communism was necessary to free us from our feelings of alienation, though some modern Marxists argue that there is no escape from alienation. Socialism, because we all own the instruments of production, theoretically makes alienation less important and less painful in our everyday lives. Marxism has generally been rejected as an economic system, but it is still used by many scholars as the basis of their critique of capitalism and contemporary consumer societies.

Alliteration

Alliteration is a rhetorical technique that attracts our attention and helps us remember advertisements by using the same letters or sounds serially. Some examples of alliteration in advertising are:

"Don't dream it. Drive it." (Jaguar)
"Discover the Doral Difference." (Doral)
"Magazines Move Millions. One Mind at a Time." (Magazine Industry)
"Top People Take the Times." (*London Times*)

Allusions

Allusions are references to events that people know about. They are useful in advertising because they take advantage of information that people already have in their heads. Thus, mentioning something like "9/11" stirs up emotions people have about that tragedy. The famous Macintosh "1984" commercial has allusions to the George Orwell novel, *1984,* and many advertisements contain allusions to myths, to the Bible, to things that famous people have said and done, famous novels and films and other works of art, and to widely known social and political events. A Samsung smart phone advertisement, "It Doesn't Take a Genius," involved an allusion to an ill-fated Apple "genius" campaign which was discontinued shortly after it began. When creators of advertising borrow themes and styles or other things from films, novels and other texts, in academic jargon this phenomenon is called "intertextuality."

Archetype

The term "archetype" comes from Jungian psychoanalytic theory. Carl Jung believed that certain themes are universal and show themselves in myths, dream, religions, and works of art. They are part of what he called our "collective unconscious" and exist independent of the personal unconscious of individuals. As Jung (1964) explains in his *Man and His Symbols:*

> What we properly call instincts are physiological urges, and are perceived by the senses. But at the same time, they also manifest themselves in fantasies and often reveal their presence only by symbolic images. These manifestations are what I call the archetypes. They are without known origin; and they reproduce themselves in any time or in any part of the world—even where transmission by direct descent or "cross fertilization" through migration must be ruled out. (Garden City, NY: Doubleday, p. 69)

Jung believed that "the hero figure is an archetype, which has existed since time immemorial" (p. 73), and that other archetypes are the myth of Paradise or of a past "golden age," when everyone lived in peaceful times and shared in abundance. Advertisers often use archetypal figures, especially heroes and heroines, because of their impact on our collective psyches and emotions.

Aristotle (Greek, 384–322 BC)

Aristotle was one of the most famous Greek philosophers. He wrote a great deal about various kinds of communication in his books such as *Poetics* and *Rhetoric,* which I deal with in my discussion of rhetoric.

Artists and other "Creatives"

There are two kinds of artists we can talk about in the advertising industry. There are the artists, art directors, and designers, who usually work with a copywriter in a creative team, and there are the models, actors and actresses, musicians, film and video makers, video editors, and all others who are involved in making print advertisements and commercials. It is these "creatives" who actually make the advertisements and commercials and other kinds of advertising we hear and see, and to a considerable degree it is the talent of their creatives that helps explain why certain advertising agencies are popular and successful. As we might expect, star artists and copywriters are very highly paid when they work in major advertising agencies since the success of the agency is dependent on their work.

Aspirational Buyers

This term refers to people who purchase products, usually with popular brand names, that help them deal with matters such as their desire to gain high status, their need for security, and their attempts to deal with their anxieties and various other needs. Thus, women who purchase Coach's mid-range handbags for $400 or other ultra-expensive handbags from other brands such as Dior can be seen as aspirational buyers. Dior handbags often cost several thousand dollars, and some brands have even more expensive handbags.

Aspirational brands of products are generally more expensive than other brands and confer a feeling of being successful on those who can afford to purchase aspirational products. There is often a range of products within an aspirational brand. Thus, for example, there are many different models of BMW, from the least expensive entry-level model to its most expensive and most aspirational model. A book by Michael J. Silverstein and Neil Fiske, *Trading Up: Why Consumers Want New Luxury Goods—and How Companies Create Them,* deals with luxury brands that have positioned themselves to

This advertisement is from Dior, an upscale company whose products are quite expensive and thus appeal to aspirational buyers. Some handbags from name brands cost between $10,000 and $20,000 dollars. Notice the use of sexuality to sell the handbag and the curious expression on the model's face. We follow the red diagonal at the bottom of the red purse down to the woman's left breast, and from there, the black diagonal down towards her vagina.

appeal to aspirational buyers. As they explain in their book (2008, New York: Portfolio, p.1):

> America's middle-market customers are trading up. They are willing, even eager, to pay premium prices for remarkable kinds of goods that we call New Luxury—products and services that possess higher levels of quality, taste, and aspiration than other goods in the category but are not so expensive so as to be out of reach.

In the book we find discussions of companies such as Belvedere vodka, Calloway golf clubs, and Victoria's Secret—brands that are aspirational in nature. These new luxury goods, the authors explain, "are always based on emotions and consumers have a much stronger emotional engagement with them than with other brands" (p. 5). They differ from what the authors describe as Old Luxury goods, such as Chanel bags and Rolls Royce automobiles, which are based on class, status, and exclusivity.

Audiences (Target)

Advertising is generally directed toward certain "target audiences," or groups of people who are most likely to use a product or service being advertised. The most desirable target audience is now held to be males between ages eighteen and forty-nine, which also is a group that is very difficult to reach by advertisers. Because so many members of this target audience watch sports, televised baseball games, football games, basketball games, and so on have become a major factor in advertising directed towards males. That explains why you see so many commercials for beer and automobiles during televised games and why the 2013 Superbowl sold out all the time for commercials. In the 2013 Superbowl, a thirty second commercial sold for almost 4 million dollars.

The target audience for medicines is much older, which explains why the news show, *60 Minutes,* has so many commercials for medicines. The average age of a viewer of that program is elderly. There may be some comfort in our knowing that we are all target audiences for some advertising agency that wants to sell things we didn't know we needed until they told us we did.

There are many books that marketers can use devoted to specific target audiences, such as the Generation X book, published by New Strategist. It publishes books on target audiences such as children, teens, Asian-Americans, and senior citizens. Advertisers are now focusing their attention on men and women who are members of generation X and generation Y since they are now purchasing entry-level Mercedes and BMW automobiles and other semi-luxury products. Marketers tend to see the world in terms of categories of consumers, such as teens, the elderly, and Asian-Americans.

Authority

One of the reasons we purchase products, such as medicines, is because of testimonials in advertising by authority figures, such as physicians, whose expertise helps us deal with anxieties we might feel about the quality or usefulness of the product. Many of these advertisements have a line such as "Ask your physician about our medicine," and these campaigns have led to physicians now being inundated by requests by their patients. Aristotle wrote about *ethos*, the credibility of certain people, as a means of convincing others about some matter. Many ads and commercials for powerful medicines also contain long lists of negative side effects the medicine may have.

The authority figures in the advertisements and commercials help people with serious medical problems deal with their anxieties about the negative side effects of the products by suggesting that the benefits outweigh the risks.

Barthes, Roland (France, 1915–1980)

Roland Barthes was a French Marxist and semiotician (see semiotics definition) who wrote many brilliant analyses of advertisements (and everything else) and influenced many semioticians and scholars in other disciplines as well. His book, *Mythologies,* deals with everything from wrestling on television to the classic French meal of steak and "frites."

Baudrillard, Jean (France, 1929–2007)

Baudrillard was a French sociologist who was an important theorist of postmodernism. He explained that reality has been replaced by what he called "hyperreality," which means that we live in a world of simulacra—that is, imitations of reality.

Berger, John (England, 1926–)

John Berger is a British Marxist who made a series of television programs on art for the British Broadcasting Corporation and wrote a book, *Ways of Seeing,* based on the series. One of the chapters in the book deals with advertising, or what Berger calls "publicity." He writes (1972, London: British Broadcasting System, pp. 131–132) about advertising/publicity:

> It proposes to each of us that we transform ourselves, or our lives, by buying something more.
>
> This more, it proposes, will make us in some way richer—even though we will be poorer for having spent our money.
>
> Publicity persuades us of such a transformation by showing us people who have apparently been transformed and are, as a result, enviable. The state of being envied is what constitutes

This Calvin Klein advertisement features a beautiful woman, who represents what John Berger describes as "glamour," and makes use of the feeling of envy women have that leads them to purchase products that they believe will make them feel glamorous and envied by others.

glamour. And publicity is the process of manufacturing glamour....Publicity is never a celebration of pleasure-in-itself. Publicity is always about the future buyer. It offers him an image of himself made glamorous by the product or opportunity it is trying to sell. The image then makes him envious of himself as he might be. Yet what makes this self-which-he-might-be enviable? The envy of others. Publicity is about social relations, not objects.

Advertising, Berger suggests, is all about personal transformations and glamour, and ultimately, is about social relations, not the things we purchase as a result of advertising. Berger adds that advertising is really about being envied by others and about our envying ourselves when, we believe, we will be transformed by purchasing something new.

Borrowed Interest

This refers to appropriating terms that are popular into advertisements to obtain what might be described as a "halo effect." In an article by Stuart Elliott in the March 25, 2013, *New York Times,* "Ads That Speak the Language of Social Media," he explains that many brands now are trying to associate themselves with social media and use terms such as "like," "social network," and "status update" to attract interest. As Elliott explains, "The appropriation of the trappings of social media for marketing purposes is an example of a tactic known as borrowed interest by which brands seek to associate themselves with elements of popular culture that are pervasive enough to be familiar to the proverbial everybody" (p. B6).

Thus, mentioning Facebook attaches a brand to the feelings a billion people have about it. Brands use borrowed interest to take advantage of holidays, events of cultural interest, and anything else they can do to attract the attention of potential customers. Many executives in advertising think borrowed interest is a crutch and reveals a lack of imagination on the part of brands using this device.

Brands

One of the most important things that advertising does is to establish identities for brands in the minds of those exposed to advertising of all kinds. This advertisement for Movado suggests it is an advanced and very modern watch, which is reflected in its elegant simplicity.

Gerald Zalman, a professor at Harvard's business school, offers some insights into the power of brands. He explains in *How Customers Think* that brands, in the fifties, attached social meanings that were prevalent to brands, but that has changed and now they help us deal with uncertainties and anxieties we have. They function as surrogate traditions because the stories which these brands tell about themselves have great meaning to people. As he writes (2003, Boston: Harvard Business School Press, pp. 231–232):

Notice the extreme simplicity of this advertisement and of the Movado watch. In American culture, upscale products often are characterized by simplicity and a formal design.

Movado watches sell from $500 up.

The meaning of a brand resides in the minds of *consumers,* not in the physical brand itself or in advertising about the brand. That is, consumers—not managers—ultimately create brand meaning. This meaning emerges from the interaction between consumers' consensus maps and their brand experiences—including exposure to brand attributes, product performance and advertising. Marketers can influence the meaning that consumers create by providing critical raw materials in the form of icons, metaphors and phrases. However, they cannot *control* consumers' manufacture of meaning.

He adds that a brand's meaning exists at different levels of a consumer's psyche: a surface meaning, which involves the physical attributes; a deeper meaning involving the psychological or social consequences of the brand; and at the deepest level, how it relates to a consumer's basic values and life goals.

Consumers, he continues, "develop coherent stories about these brands, and those stories are encoded in their memories." Notice that Zalman discusses three levels of meaning for consumers—and these three levels correspond to Freud's theories about the conscious, the preconscious, and the unconscious.

In addition, Zalman discusses the matter of "meaning," a topic that is basic to semiotic theory and the writings of Ferdinand de Saussure and C. S. Peirce. He deals with both psychoanalytic theory and semiotics in his book.

In an article I wrote, "The Branded Self," I discuss the role that branding plays in the way we create our "selves."

The model in this Guess advertisement is looking at herself in a mirror, suggesting an element of narcissism that is connected to the way consumers focus on themselves and the brands they use as a means of establishing an identity. She is, curiously, wearing gloves while applying lipstick.

We can make a distinction between three levels of the self: the *persona* or mask—that is, the public self which is the branded self. At a level below that is the *privata*, the private self that we do not display to others and find difficulty in accessing most of the time. And at the lowest level is the *privatissima*, the self that we cannot ever know, but which plays a role in shaping our other selves. It may be that brands speak to something in this privatissima that then manifests itself in the brands we purchase to create our personas, our public branded selves.

The fact that the self is so often defined by the collection of brands a person selected to create a public identity, and the fact that people change their branded selves, suggests that the concept of "the self" is a modernist one, based on a notion that a self is somehow lasting and coherent in its stylistic formation. The branded self, which argues that selves are based on the selection of brands that people think suit themselves, suggests a postmodern perspective on the self—one in which eclecticism rules....

There are no static selves in postmodern societies, as people are continually reinventing themselves, and since this is done through our fashion and various props, it means that postmodern selves are based upon the continual consumption of clothes, cell phones, MP3 players (such as iPods), tablet computers and other items that we use to influence the way people perceive us. Lady Gaga, who described herself as a "student of fame," would be an example of the way we use fashion and props to continually reinvent ourselves. In the end, it is the dollar or other currencies that provide postmodern selves and societies with a kind of grounding. (*American Sociologist,* 42[2], pp. 232–237)

Brands, then, play a major role in the way we think about ourselves and the way we present ourselves to others. Whether there is something we can call a "self" in postmodern societies where we are constantly changing our selves is a question that philosophers continue to debate. We may keep changing ourselves, but for many people, their brands don't change because of the topic I discuss next, brand extensions.

Brands use their popularity and status as means of extending their range. Here we see that Mont Blanc, which is known for the quality of their pens, now sells watches. There is what we might call a "halo" effect that becomes transferred from their pens to all the other Mont Blanc branded products.

Brand Extensions

Once a company has a well-known and valued brand it can capitalize on the aura the brand has in the public's mind by manufacturing other products. Thus, a company like Ralph Lauren that began by selling clothing now sells perfume, sunglasses, watches, and many other products whose selling power is connected to the cachet of the Ralph Lauren brand. The same applies to the German pen manufacturer, Mont Blanc, which has extended its brand from very fine and expensive pens into watches and fragrances—a classic example of brand extension. Well-known brands have a "halo effect" in which the brand's qualities and reputation for one product are extended to its other products. This is a great comfort to people who have anxieties about their purchases.

This halo effect is also at work in upscale stores like Tiffany, Neiman Marcus, and Saks Fifth Avenue in which the brand of the establishment means "quality" in people's minds. In my discussion of commodity aesthetics, I deal with the theories of Wolfgang Fritz Haug, who writes about the way department stores and other emporia have transformed themselves into venues for entertainment in which people can act out their fantasies as they buy things.

Brand Community

Apple is an outstanding example of a brand that has created a "community" around its products and services. Many computer users identify themselves as "Apple" people and are proud of using Apple products and loyal to Apple in their choice of other products, such as smart phones and tablets. Before the popularity of the iPhone and other products, users of Mac computers formed a relatively small community who felt threatened by the huge mass of PC users and also had mild contempt for them since Apple products, so the Apple Brand community felt, were so superior. Now the Apple community can purchase iPhones, iPads, iPods, Macintosh computers, and many other Apple products.

The Apple brand community has, I would suggest, an element of compulsion permeating it. Maybe the Apple brand community even has elements of being a cult. Once you purchase an Apple product, you are most likely to purchase other Apple products, and there is an element of subtle compulsion at work. In the "1984" Macintosh commercial, IBM was the "big brother" figure. Now, I would suggest, the new "big brother" is Apple.

Brand Image

A brand image involves what the brand projects to people about its quality and value. An image, used this way, deals with perceptions people have about some brand and its various products. The image that a Rolls Royce has in people's minds is quite different from the image they have of a Porsche or a Maserati and of the kind of people who prefer Rolls Royces to Maseratis. A brand's image, then, plays a role in choices consumers make and they often devote a considerable amount of time and energy in making decisions about the proper brand to purchase. For example, a friend of mine who is a dean in a university in Hong Kong told me he asked many people there about the brand and model of a car he should purchase when he took the job and moved to Hong Kong.

Martin Mayer quotes a speech by David Ogilvy about brand images that comes to the point. Ogilvy said (quoted in Mayer's *Madison Avenue U.S.A.*, 1967, New York: Pocket Books, p. 36):

> Every advertisement must be considered as a contribution to the complex symbol which is the brand image....I am astonished to find how many manufacturers, even among the new generation, believe that women can be persuaded by *logic* and *argument* to buy one brand in preference to another—even when the two brands are technically identical....The manufacturers who dedicate their advertising to building the most favorable image, the most sharply defined *personality* for their brands, are the ones who will get the largest share of the market at the highest profit—in the long run.

What Ogilvy reminds us is that most purchases are the result of emotional attachments we make to products, not their technical qualities. It is images that sell—in particular, brand images to which people have become attached, with which they empathize, and which they trust.

Branding

In his book, *Shoptimism: Why the American Consumer Will Keep on Buying No Matter What,* Lee Eisenberg has a chapter titled "You Are What You Buy." He discusses some of the books he's purchased on the subject of why people buy things and writes (2009, New York: Free Press, p. 166):

> Most of these books, having posited the notion that you are what you buy, expand on it by noting how our adoration of specific

brands bonds us to others with the same preferences. We share loyalty (bordering on obsession) to VW Beetles or Vermont Casting woodstoves. These allegiances herd us into "brand tribes," a fashionable "Sell Side" term these days. Brands, these books further observe, have personalities—they're human, sort of, with distinct personality traits to which we buddy up.

It is the advertising campaigns that help give brands their distinctive personalities and help "brand communities" to form.

In her article, "Semiotics and Strategic Brand Management," Laura R. Oswald discusses the role of semiotics in creating brands. She writes:

Over the past ten years or so, brand strategy researchers have come to recognize the importance of brand communication in building and sustaining brand equity, the value attached to a brand name or log that supersedes product attributes and differentiates brands in the competitive arena....The contribution of brand meanings and perceptions to profitability—the Coca Cola brand is valued at over $70 billion—testifies to the power of symbolic representation to capture the hearts and minds of consumers by means of visual, audio, and verbal signs. The semiotic—or symbolic—dimension of brands is therefore instrumental for building awareness, positive associations, and long-term customer loyalty, and contributes to trademark ownership and operational advantages such as channel and media clout. Consequently, managing brand equity means managing brand *semiotics*. (www.media.illinois.edu/advertising/semiotics_oswald.pdf)

She suggests that more than anything else, it is semiotic theory that enables us to understand what brands are, how they work, and the role they play in consumer decision making.

Archaeologists Andrew Bevan and David Wengrow offer us a historical perspective on branding. In a book they edited, *Cultures of Commodity Branding,* they write (2010, Walnut Creek, CA: Left Coast Press, p. 12):

> Most people are aware and talk about commodity branding on the assumption that it is the product of modern capitalist markets, and that we therefore know quite intuitively what it involves.... In their contribution to *The Social Economy of Consumption* (1989), Hamilton and Lei convincingly argued that a complex system of commodity branding—applied to goods such as rice, tea, wine, scissors, and medicines—had existed in late imperial China, where it can be traced back to the Song dynasty of the 10th century.

Bevan and Wengrow argue, then, that branding is actually a very old phenomenon and not tied to capitalism and modernity. This is because, let me suggest, there is in people a natural tendency to differentiate among things, and this inevitably leads to various kinds of branding.

Brand Planners

I spent three weeks at Goldberg, Moser, O'Neill a few years ago and interviewed a brand manager there, Yvonne Yarnold. What follows is part of that interview, which offers insights into the work of brand planners (from my book, *The Agent in the Agency,* 2003, Cresskill, NJ: Hampton Press, pp. 95–96):

> I had written about print advertisements and commercials in the past...but always as an interpreter or critic looking at the final product...and trying to figure out how the ad generated meaning, what effects it might have had on people, and what it reflected about society and culture. Yvonne offered an interesting analogy: "You can think of me as being like an architect," she said. "I translate the desires of a person who wants to have a house built into a plan for a house that works." Her job, as I understand things, involves helping clients determine what they

really want or, in some cases, finding out what would be best for them. This is done by developing a creative brief, which takes the desires and needs of the client into account and describes what the advertising will do. She explained that there are three disciplines involved when dealing with clients:

The Brand Planner at the agency thinks "my consumer." The Creative people in the agency think "my creation" (the ad or commercial). The Account people of the agency think "my brand."

What has to be done, she suggested, is to create an impression about the brand in the minds and hearts of people...create a personality for the product by giving it attributes, a personality... using copy, art, photographs and carrying that personality through all marketing communications vehicles, such as the logo and packaging.

This interview offers us valuable insights into the way brand planners work and their role in advertising agencies. I noticed that people at the agency worked very hard and that there was a constant aura of crisis that permeated the place. As one executive there told me, "I'm so busy I don't have time to think when I'm in the office. I have to do my thinking when I'm home."

C

Celebrities

Celebrities are used frequently in advertising because people know about them and often want to imitate their behavior. A French scholar, René Girard, has a theory he calls "mimetic desire" that argues people want to imitate ("mimesis" means "imitation") the desire of movie stars and other celebrities, which leads to people purchasing products the celebrities buy, supposedly use—and sell in commercials and in print advertisements. Many people identify with celebrities and want to imitate them.

Claritas's 66 Groups of Americans

There are, according to Claritas, sixty-six different groups of Americans who form target audiences for advertisers based on their zip codes and things like magazines they read and television programs they like. Claritas argues that "birds of a feather flock together," which means that advertisers can fashion messages directed towards the members of each group or cluster of consumers (or similar groups) that will resonate with them. An advertisement directed at wealthy "Upper Crust" groups will probably also be effective with affluent "Blue Blood Estates" and "Movers and Shakers" but not with "Shotguns and Pickups" or "Big City Blues," who are at the bottom of the financial totem pole.

An English semiotician I know in advertising told me that he thinks the Claritas 66 group typology is irrelevant. "Anyone with a decent head of his or her shoulders should be able to figure out how to reach target audiences," he said. Claritas argues that since there are these sixty-six diverse and distinctive groups that advertisers want to reach, they ultimately have to employ Claritas, since it knows a great deal about each of them. The same would apply to all typologies that marketers create—their ultimate purpose is to have proprietary information that they can sell to advertising agencies to help them sell to target audiences.

Close-Ups

Close-Ups are images of only a person's face or part of a person's body. There are extreme close-ups (which I deal with later) in which we might only see a woman's lips or an eye, and there are all kinds of other shots, from medium shots, which signify personal relationships, to extreme long distance shots, which signify social relationships and gaining a sense of one's place. Each kind of shot, then, communicates a different message to people viewing the advertisement or commercial. People learn the meaning of these

This is a close-up of a person which shows his face and part of his shoulders. Close-ups are useful for advertisers because they facilitate inspection and can show a product they are selling with a considerable amount of detail. Ads like this might also suggest the kind of person who wears Dolce & Gabbana.

shots from constant exposure to them and the events that transpire in the texts to which they are exposed.

Some critics of advertising have been devoting attention to the recent trend in which only parts of models' bodies—generally women—are shown. This suggests that only certain parts of women are significant and is a reflection of the depersonalization and dehumanization that characterizes modern societies and, in particular, the way women are thought about and treated.

Cognitive Dissonance

Cognitive dissonance can be defined as feelings of discomfort that occur when we are presented with advertisements and commercials that run counter to our basic values and beliefs. People try to avoid experiencing cognitive dissonance and seek, instead, advertisements that reinforce their basic beliefs and values and, after they have purchased something, convince them that they made a good choice.

Commodities

A commodity can be seen as the opposite of a brand. Commodities are products without an advertised brand name or, in the case of foods, with the brand of the supermarket or supermarket chain—that is, a "store brand." Because store brand foods and products don't spend money on advertising, they are less expensive than brand-name products. But many consumers, especially consumers who are price sensitive and thus concerned about what things cost, purchase them to save money. There is a widespread notion that store brand products aren't as good as brand name products, but that is generally not the case.

Archaeologists Andrew Bevan and David Wengrow offer an insight into the nature of commodities in their introduction to their book, *Cultures of Commodity Branding*. They write (2010, Walnut Creek, CA: Left Coast Press, p. 15):

In a seminal piece on the social construction of value, the anthropologist Igor Kopytoff (1986) argued that commodities are not things in themselves but rather situational entities: elements of material culture (or persons) that have become temporarily enmeshed within a particular set of social and moral codes; codes that determine the character and pace of their circulation.... Kopytoff also observed that the production of commodities is "a cultural and cognitive process: commodities must not only be produced materially as things, but also culturally marked as being a certain kind of thing.

What Kopytoff is arguing is that what they call commodities are objects whose identity and value are not natural but socially constructed. And it is advertising that plays the most prominent role, I would suggest, in "social constructing" the meaning of various brands of commodities. The authors are using the term "commodity" to stand for any kind of object, in contrast to the way I have been using it in this book to stand for a non-advertised product.

Commodity Aesthetics

A German Marxist, Wolfgang Fritz Haug (1936–), has written two books on the subject of commodity aesthetics: *Critique of Commodity Aesthetics: Appearance, Sexuality and Advertising in Capitalist Society* (1971) and *Commodity Aesthetics, Ideology & Culture* (1987). His thesis is that the aesthetic qualities of commodities are now increasingly important in selling them. That explains why stores have become beautified and now function as theatre-like entities in which consumers play out their fantasies. Think, for example, of the iPhone and other Apple products, in which design elements are an important part of the appeal they have. And think, also, about the aesthetics of Apple stores and of other upscale stores. As Haug explains in his *Critique of Commodity Aesthetics: Appearance, Sexuality, and Advertising in Capitalist Society* (1971, Minneapolis: University of Minnesota Press, pp. 68–69) in which he quotes from a book, *The Key to the Consumer,* by the director of a very successful department store, Globus:

> The commodities are no longer to be displayed in their traditional categories "but should be arranged thematically to fulfill the needs and the dreams of the buyer." One must not confront the buyer brusquely with a commodity but "guide them into the 'entertainment'."...The exhibition of commodities, their inspection, the act of purchase, and all the associated moments, are integrated into the concept of one theatrical total work of art which plays on the public's willingness to buy. Thus the salesroom is designed as a stage, purpose-built to convey entertainment to its audience that will stimulate a heightened desire to spend. "On this stage the sale is initiated. The stage is the most important element in sales promotion."

From Haug's perspective, products and their advertising agencies mount a two pronged attack on the consumer: first, the commodities or objects are made beautiful or aesthetically desirable and thus have a powerful emotional (and perhaps erotic) appeal, and second, the stores are redesigned as beautiful entertainment venues where consumers can play out their fantasies.

On the cover of Haug's book we see a flock of pigeons that are eating grain that spells out Coca-Cola. Haug wonders—each of the pigeons is pursuing its own interests, but without realizing it, these pigeons are functioning as tools of the Coca-Cola Company. Are we all, Haug asks, pawns who have the illusion that we move ourselves when, in reality, our moves are ultimately determined by some great chess player in the sky or the advertising agencies that work for the chess player?

Communication Models

Advertising is a specialized kind of communication which seeks to persuade those exposed to advertisements to purchase products and services. It is useful to know something about the process of communication, which has been dealt with in a number of models of communication. I define "model" here as an abstract representation of some process of interest. The most useful model for our purpose was made by the linguist Roman Jakobson (1896–1982), who offered a model that covered what he described as the basic six elements in speech acts and communication in general.

Context

Message

Sender • • • • • • • • • • • • • • • • • Receiver

Contact (Medium)

Code

Jakobson's model involves a sender sending a message (some kind of information) to a receiver. The message is transmitted by a code (such as the English language) using a contact (or medium, such as speech). The context in which the sender sends messages plays an important role in helping the receiver make sense of the message. A message such as "pass the hypodermic needle" means one thing in a dark alley and another thing in a hospital room.

In Jakobson's model, messages have a number of functions. The most common is the *referential function*, which relates to the surroundings in which speakers and receivers find themselves. There are other functions, such as *emotive functions*, which involve the sender expressing feelings, and *poetic functions*, which involve using literary devices, such as metaphors, similes, and word choice, that give a message its tone and distinctive qualities (known as "voice"). Jakobson's model shows that communication is a complicated matter that involves a number of different processes.

If we apply Jakobson's model to advertising, we find that advertisers are senders who use various media to send messages (in the form of print advertisements and television commercials) hoping to reach certain receivers (target audiences) using emotive and poetic functions, among other things, and hoping the receivers will decode the messages the way the advertisers want them to. Thus, we can modify Jakobson's model and apply it to advertising:

Context (TV show, newspaper, magazine)

Message (advertisement or commercial)

Sender (ad agency) · · · · · · · Receiver (target audience)

Contact (radio, TV, print)

Code (English language, images)

It's one thing to understand how the process of communication works. It's another thing to create advertisements and commercials that are effective.

Comparison Advertisements

Comparisons are odious because there usually is an element of criticism as an important element or subtext to comparisons. Products such as computers and cell phones often use comparisons to try to show that they are superior to their competitors. In these ads you often find charts that list the attributes of the product making the advertisements and compare them with the attributes of products offered by its competitors.

In 2012 there was an interesting advertisement for Samsung smart phones, "It Doesn't Take A Genius," in which Samsung alluded to a failed Apple campaign and compared the technical specifications of its Galaxy phone and iPhones. The Samsung phone had many more specifications than iPhones, as one might imagine. Technical devices and gizmos often use logic in their advertising—in this case, comparisons and contrasts.

Concepts

I make a distinction between concepts and theories. Theories, as I understand the term, are overarching explanations of how our minds work, how our economies work, how the physical sciences work, what motivates people, and that kind of thing. Concepts are ideas within theories that deal with topics of interest. Thus, in Freudian psychoanalytic theory, there are numerous concepts he uses to explain human behavior, such as the Unconscious, the Oedipus complex, narcissism, defense mechanisms, and the Id, Ego, and Superego. Many people who work in the creative side of the advertising industry are aware of Freud's ideas and try to use them to motivate people who watch or listen to advertisements and commercials. Marxism has many concepts, such as alienation, the ruling class, class warfare, and materialism. We can say, without being too simplistic, that all theories have concepts which explain how the theory functions and apply the theory to people and to society.

The following chart shows the relationship that exists between theories and concepts as I interpret things. I use psychoanalytic theory and Marxism as examples of the relationship between theories and concepts, but I could use other theories as well:

Theory	**Psychoanalytic Theory**	**Marxism**
Concepts	Unconscious	Class conflict
	Oedipus complex	Alienation
	Id/Ego/Superego	False consciousness
	Defense mechanisms	Consumer cultures

We can see, then, that concepts help us understand what theories deal with and why they are so important. I have only listed some of the more important concepts found in each theory; in reality, there are many others that I could have listed.

As I define it, a concept is an idea, such as the Oedipus complex, that is part of some theory, such as the psychoanalytic theory. Concepts show how a theory explains something or some kind of behavior. Thus "ambivalence" is a psychoanalytic theory that explains how we can like and hate someone or something at the same time. Concepts, as I define them, are parts of theories that help us understand behavior. In the advertising world, concepts have a different meaning. In advertising a concept refers to the basic idea behind an advertisement or advertising campaign.

Marshall McLuhan defined concepts in his *The Mechanical Bride: The Folklore of Industrial Man* as follows: "Concepts are provisional affairs for apprehending reality; their value is in the grip they provide. This book, therefore, tries to present representative aspects of the reality and a wide range of ideas for taking hold of it" (1951/1967, Boston: Beacon, p. vi).

And that is what I've done in this dictionary. I offer you a "wide range of ideas" for understanding advertising and its role in society.

Let me offer an example of how concepts work. Suppose you know someone who washes his hands 200 times each day. There is a concept from psychoanalytic theory that explains this kind of behavior—obsessive compulsive behavior. So there are three levels that we can deal with here:

Action	Washing hands 200 times a day
Concept	Obsessive compulsive behavior
Theory	Psychoanalytic theory

The concept explains the behavior and is part of some theory. The concepts I use in this book help explain different aspects of advertising and come from a variety of theorists such as Marshall McLuhan, Vance Packard, Max Weber, Roland Barthes, Jean Baudrillard, Henri Lefebvre, and Sigmund Freud.

I also make a distinction between concepts and jargon or what we might call "Ad Speak," which has hundreds of terms that people in the advertising industry use. Advertising jargon generally doesn't have the theoretical significance or explanatory power that concepts have and doesn't help us understand how advertising works and what its role is in contemporary societies.

Connotation and Denotation

Semioticians make a distinction between connotation and denotation. The term "connotation" is derived from the Latin *connotare* which means "to mark along with." Connotation deals with the image the product has in people's minds, with emotions the product generates, and with the cultural meanings that are attached to words and objects and to other forms of communication. "Denotation," on the other hand, describes the physical attributes of some object and refers to the literal meanings of words and other phenomena. It comes from the Latin word *denotare*, "to note." Thus, the denotations of an object like a Barbie Doll are that it was created in 1959 and originally was 11.5 inches high, was 5.25 inches at the bust, 3.0 inches at the waist, and 4.25 inches at the hips. The connotations of a Barbie Doll are that it teaches girls to focus their attention on themselves and their role as consumers rather than it being a rehearsal for motherhood, which is the function of traditional baby dolls for young girls.

Denotation is the opposite of connotation. Denotation deals with the specific physical attributes of a product. Thus, a Barbie Doll's denotation is that it is so many inches long, has a certain color hair, and so forth. The connotation of Barbie Dolls involves the role they play in the social development of little girls—moving them away from traditional dolls, which prepare them for marriage and taking care of babies, to a new identity as courtesan and consumer.

CPM (Cost Per Thousand)

Advertisers used CPM (M stands for a thousand) to determine what it costs to expose a thousand members of a target audience to its advertisements and commercials. CPM is a measure of effectiveness. It might cost 3 million dollars to run a thirty second commercial on the Superbowl, but that may turn out to be less expensive, on a cost per thousand basis, than paying 300,000 dollars to broadcast a commercial on a television show with a relatively small audience.

Consumer Cultures

According to Marxists, capitalism survives by distracting members of the working class from paying attention to the ways they are exploited and focusing their energy on personal consumption, leading to consumer cultures. It is their alienation from themselves and society that directs their energy. Success in consumer cultures is measured by how many possessions a person has. In consumer cultures, lifestyle is all important, and people focus their energies on their lifestyles and the various products that demonstrate one's life style. The public sphere is neglected since personal expenditures are the focus, not public investments in institutions. It is advertising that plays a major role in shaping our desires for products and services which, ultimately, we take as a sign that we are loved by God.

David Potter, in his classic work, *People of Plenty*, points out that advertising not only has economic consequences, it also shapes our values (1954, Chicago: University of Chicago Press, p. 188):

> The most important effects of this powerful institution are not upon the economics of our distributive system; they are upon the values of our society. If the economic effect is to make the purchaser like what he buys, the social effect is, in a parallel but broader sense, to make the individual like what he gets— to enforce already existing attitudes, to diminish the range and variety of choices, and in terms of abundance, to exalt the materialistic virtues of consumption.

It's a curious thing that while advertising, as an industry, is often quite avant-garde and bold in the techniques it uses, its impact is a conservative one—to maintain, to the degree possible, the status quo. One reason companies advertise is to maintain their market share; if they can increase it, all the better. In *Consumer Culture and Postmodernism,* Mike Featherstone explains the importance of "life-style" in contemporary consumer societies (1991, Thousand Oaks, CA: Sage, p. 86):

Rather than unreflexively adopting a lifestyle, through tradition or habit, the new heroes of consumer culture make lifestyle a life project and display their individuality and sense of style in the particularity of the assemblage of goods, clothes, practices, experiences, appearance and bodily dispositions they design together into a lifestyle. The modern individual within consumer culture is made conscious that he speaks not only with his clothes, but also with his home, furnishings, decorations, car and other activities which are to be read and classified in terms of the presence and absence of taste. The preoccupation with customizing a lifestyle and a stylistic self-consciousness are not just to be found among the young and the affluent; consumer culture publicity [advertising] suggests that we all have room for self-improvement and self-expression whatever our age or class origins.

It is advertising that "teaches" us about the world of consumer goods—what is fashionable and "hot" or, maybe even better for some people, "cool."

Collective Unconscious

According to Carl G. Jung, there is something we can describe as a "collective unconscious" which is not learned but is part of all human beings and manifests itself in the kinds of heroes we create, certain themes that continually appear in our dreams, and archetypes that are universal. As he writes in *Man and His Symbols* (1968, Garden City, NY: Doubleday, p. 64):

> We do not assume that each new-born animal creates its own instincts as an individual acquisition, and we must not suppose that human individuals invent their specific human ways with every new birth. Like the instincts, the collective thought patterns of the human mind are innate and inherited. They function, when the occasion arises, in more or less the same way in all of us.

If this is the case, and Jung's notions about a collective unconscious are very controversial, advertising agencies that can tap into the collective thought patterns should be more effective than agencies that do not know about them or do not use them well. For many psychologists, Jung's notions about collective thought patterns and a collective unconscious may be interesting but are theories which have not been validated by science.

Copywriters

Copywriters are part of the "creative" teams in advertising agencies that think up the slogans and write the material (copy) found in print ads and the dialogue in television commercials. They usually work in a team with an art director to create ads of all kinds for all media. It is the cleverness of copywriters that attracts our attention and, when the advertisement is successful, stimulates desire and leads to our purchasing whatever it is that is being advertised. Some copywriters are freelancers and work for themselves in their own one-man agencies or work for large agencies on a temporary basis. Copywriters are people who have a way with words. Consider the copy in this advertisement for Living Proof Hydracel by Geminesse.

The first paragraph of the advertisement reads as follows:

There is
a fountain of youth.
It's called water.

Nature has been telling us this forever. Water keeps a rose fresh and beautiful. A peach juicy. All living things, living. Including your skin. The millions of cells in your skin contain water. This water pillows and cushions your skin, making it soft and young-looking. But, for a lot of reasons, cells become unable to hold water. And the water escapes your skin. (If you'll forgive us, think of a prune drying up and you'll know the whole story.)

The copywriter who wrote this advertisement scares readers by offering a very graphic image. When women are young their skin

This advertisement contains a veiled threat to women and suggests that their youthfulness and femininity are connected to using the correct moisturizer—Living Proof Cream Hydracel by Geminesse. If they don't, their complexions will change from looking like a peach to looking like a prune.

There is a fountain of youth. It's called water.

Nature has been telling us this forever.
Water keeps a rose fresh and beautiful. A peach, juicy. All living things, living. Including your skin.
The millions of cells in your skin contain water. This water pillows and cushions your skin, making it soft and young-looking.
But, for a lot of reasons, cells become unable to hold enough water. And the water escapes from your skin.
(If you'll forgive us, think of a prune drying up and you know the whole story.)
Now, moisturizers have helped but only up to a point.

The truth about moisturizers.

Most people think a moisturizer literally puts moisture into your skin.
Not true. (Your skin has all the water it needs. Holding it there is the problem.)
An average moisturizer holds the water in by blocking its escape.
But, unfortunately, this does not affect your cells' ability to retain water. This is where we come in.
We are Living Proof by Geminesse. And our breakthrough is Cream Hydracel.

Hydracel: nature's helper.

The name Hydracel tells you what we're all about: water and cell.
Cream Hydracel actually helps the cellular tissues retain water.
We let nature do the work, not heavy creams. And this can make all the difference.
Your skin will breathe and start to recover its water-holding power.
And your face will feel softer and look younger, naturally.
It's as simple as that.

Our promise isn't a promise. It's a fact.

After just three days with Cream Hydracel, your skin will feel softer.
After a few weeks, your skin will actually look younger.
And it only gets better. Because Cream Hydracel helps to restore—and maintain—the natural water balance in your skin.
And this is what helps keep skin soft and young-looking.
Nature gave you a fountain of youth. Cream Hydracel keeps it flowing.

LIVING PROOF
Cream Hydracel
by GEMINESSE

is soft and smooth, like a juicy peach. But when they get old, their skin loses water and resembles a plum that has dried up and become full of wrinkles—a prune. Women can prevent this from happening, the copy reminds us, by using Hydracel. The copywriter has offered readers very graphic images and a stark comparison: peaches and prunes. To my mind, this is a brilliant example of copywriting which terrorizes women by suggesting that unless they use the product, so they can remain "young looking" and sexually attractive, their skin will resemble a wrinkled old prune. It taps into unconscious fears and anxieties women feel about getting old and no longer being beautiful and therefore, they believe, becoming undesirable and unworthy of love.

Creative Directors

Creative directors are the people at advertising agencies who are ultimately responsible for the way advertisements and commercials turn out, since they assign teams of copywriters and artists to work on certain products and services and oversee their progress. They usually have a great deal of experience as copywriters, designers, and art directors, which enables them to work on getting new business for the agency, to develop and oversee advertising campaigns for clients, and to participate in agency "pitches" to potential new clients. The ability of the creative director to inspire confidence in potential new clients for the agency is connected to both the quality of work of the agency and the concepts the creative directors and other members of the agency come up with to convince potential clients to use the agency.

Culture

There are hundreds of different definitions of the term "culture," which is a central concept in anthropology. Generally speaking, culture stands for the ideas, beliefs, values, behavior patterns, and customs that are transmitted from generation to generation. Culture is reflected in the arts, both elite (operas, ballets, serious novels) and popular (television, films, sports and so-called mass mediated culture), and in the objects a society produces (that's called "material culture"). Advertisers can use widely-held cultural beliefs and notions in trying to convince people to purchase products and services.

Stuart Hall, a British communication scholar, explains why we've become so interested in culture in the introduction to his edited book, *Representation: Cultural Representations and Signifying Practices* (1997, London: Sage, pp. 2–3):

> What has come to be called "the cultural turn" in the social and human sciences, especially in cultural studies and the sociology of culture, has tended to emphasize the importance of *meaning* to the definition of culture. Culture, it is argued, is not so much a set of *things*—novels and paintings or TV programmes and comics—as a process, a set of *practices*. Primarily, culture is

concerned with the production and the exchange of meanings—the "giving and taking of meaning"—between the members of a society or group. To say that two people belong to the same culture is to say that they interpret the world in roughly the same ways and can express themselves, their thoughts and feelings about the world, in ways which will be understood by each other….It is participants in a culture who give meaning to people, objects and events. Things "in themselves" rarely if ever have one, single, fixed and unchanging meaning.

This means that learning how to interpret and analyze advertising, one of our culture's most important genres of mass-mediated texts, is a way of learning about our culture and, indirectly, because we are members of this culture, about ourselves. Hall's perspective is essentially semiotic, focusing on the importance of signifying processes and meaning. Academics in a number of disciplines and copywriters and art directors in advertising agencies both wrestle with this question: How do people find meaning in texts and the images, narratives, and words in commercials? People are extremely complicated, and finding ways to understand the way their minds work and the effects of emotional experiences on their decision making is a perennial problem.

Culture Code

Clotaire Rapaille is a French anthropologist, psychoanalyst, and marketing consultant who wrote a bestselling book, *The Culture Code: An Ingenious Way to Understand Why People Around the World Live and Buy as They Do*. He argues that during the first seven years of our lives we all become "imprinted" with the national codes in the societies in which we grow up. Imprints are combinations of experiences we have and the emotions that accompany them. As he explains: "Once an imprint occurs, it strongly conditions our thought processes and shapes our future actions. Each imprint helps make us who we are. The combination of imprints defines us" (2006, New York: Broadway Books, p. 6).

We must recognize that these imprints influence us at the unconscious level. His work, he writes, involved him searching for our imprints so he could decode "elements of our culture to discover the emotions and meanings attached to them" (pp. 10–11). Most of the imprinting is done in children during the first seven years of their lives because "emotion is the central force for children under the age of seven" (p. 21). Early in his career he spent time searching for the codes "hidden within the unconscious of every culture," by which he really means nations.

He offers an example of decoding cultures in his discussion of cheese (p. 25):

> The French Code for cheese is ALIVE. This makes perfect sense when one considers how the French choose and store cheese. They go to a cheese shop and poke and prod the cheeses, smelling them to learn their ages. When they choose one, they take it home and store it is a cloche (a bell-shape cover with little holes to allow air in and keep insects out). The American Code for cheese, on the other hand, is DEAD. Again, this makes sense in context. Americans "kill" their cheese through pasteurization (unpasteurized cheeses are not allowed into the country), select hunks of cheese that have been prewrapped—mummified if you will—in plastic (like body bags), and store it, still wrapped airtight, in a morgue known as a refrigerator.

Rapaille's use of language is important. Americans "mummify" their cheeses and store them in "morgues." The point to recognize is that from Rapaille's perspective and from a semiotic perspective, cultures can be seen as full of different kinds of codes which the semiotician must learn how to decode. Knowing the codes that shape people's behavior is a key job of advertisers, because when they can make advertisements that connect with these codes and use them, their advertisements will most likely be more powerful and effective. We can suggest that advertisers attempt to find and use the culture codes that shape our thinking and emotions...and ultimately our behavior.

de Certeau, Michel (France, 1925–1986)

Michel de Certeau was a Jesuit scholar and influential French culture critic who applied psychoanalytic theory, philosophy, and other theories to his study of everyday life and the role of the media in society.

Decoding

Decoding refers to the process we use to make sense of words, images, and communication in general. Let's take the following example: John says "Do you want to get a cup of coffee?" to Mary. To simplify matters, communication occurs, as Jakobson explains, when someone, a sender, encodes a message and transmits it using some medium to a receiver, who decodes the message. Thus, a conversation involves where a conversation is taking place (context), a person (the sender), using the code (English), speaks to someone (the receiver), who decodes the message.

Context	Location of conversation
Message	Want to get a cup of coffee?
Sender	John
Receiver	Mary
Medium	Speech
Code	English

This is a model of a widely known theory of communication that was elaborated by a celebrated linguist, Roman Jakobson. He pointed out that context often plays an important role in our decoding a message. The sentence above, about getting a cup of coffee, is a very simple one and easy to decode, if you know English.

Advertisements and television commercials are much more complicated texts and often are not decoded the way the senders, the copywriters and artists, want them to be decoded. Semioticians call mistakes by the receivers of advertisements and commercials "aberrant decodings." According to Umberto Eco, an Italian semiotician, people aberrantly decode communications most of the time, which means that viewers of commercials, for example, frequently don't "get" the message, or they interpret the commercial in an incorrect manner.

The French culture critic Michel de Certeau also suggests that members of audiences do not all interpret the messages they receive the same way and often manipulate these messages for their own benefit. Thus, the "weak" find ways to prevent the "strong" (in this case advertisers) from manipulating them. As he explains in *The Practice of Everyday Life* (1984, Berkeley: University of California Press, p. 169):

> Recent analyses show that "every reading modifies its object," that (as Borges already pointed out) "one literature differs from another less by its text than by the way it is read," and that a system of verbal or iconic signs is a reservoir of forms to which the reader must give a meaning....The reader takes neither the position of the author nor an author's position. He invents in texts something different from what they "intended." He detaches them from their (lost or accessory) origin. He combines their fragments and creates something un-known in the space organized by their capacity for allowing an indefinite plurality of meanings.

De Certeau suggests that people who are exposed to texts, and we can include advertising here, don't always respond to them the way the advertising agencies that created these texts think they will. Readers must give meaning to advertisements and, if de Certeau is correct, people exposed to advertising create their own meanings. This argument is similar to the one made by reader response theorists who are discussed later in this book. Every advertisement and commercial is susceptible to many different interpretations.

The question we must ask is this: How different are the readings? Even if the interpretations each person makes of an advertisement are different, do people exposed to these texts still get most of the message? If people interpreted every advertisement or commercial in wildly different ways, the advertising industry wouldn't be as successful as it has been with so many campaigns, people wouldn't understand novels or respond to films and television programs the way they do. De Certeau's main point is that people can resist the media they consume and use it for their own purposes. We are not "brainwashed" by our exposure to advertising...or, at least, not to the degree that advertisers would like us to be. De Certeau gives audiences power in dealing with commercials.

Dichter, Ernest (Vienna, 1907–1991)

Ernest Dichter is known as the father of motivation research, and his work was very influential in the advertising industry. He was educated at the University of Paris and received a PhD from the University of Vienna. Dichter's work applies psychoanalytic theory to discerning how people feel about products at the three levels of consciousness: the conscious level, the subconscious level, and the unconscious level, which is the most important level for motivation researchers. If you know what motivates people, you have a better notion of how to make advertisements that will appeal to them, especially at the unconscious level—appeals which they are unaware of but which may shape their behavior.

As Dichter explained in his book, *The Strategy of Desire:* "Many of our daily decisions are governed by motivations over which we have no control and of which we are often quite unaware" (1960, New Brunswick, NJ: Transaction, p. 12). So it is our unconscious desires that ultimately shape our behavior in various areas, including buying things. What marketing research does is discover these "unconscious" desires and feelings we have about products so advertisers can use them in an attempt to shape our behavior. Dichter also pointed out in his book that motivation research could be used for causes such as lessening anti-Semitism and racism in societies, and getting people to donate blood or stop smoking.

This Ungaro advertisement is highly stylized and extremely simple, suggesting elegance and refinement. We don't see the face of the model, so she could be anyone. She is wearing a beautiful gown that has a classic look to it. And we only see a touch of her cleavage. The language of the advertisement is French, which can be tied to notions people have about the French being sophisticated and sexy. The name of the perfume, Diva, also is highly suggestive.

Differentiation

Branding's main goal is that of differentiation—distinguishing a product's brand from other bands and from a brand's mortal enemy, store brands and commodities. Brands differentiate themselves from other brands by using logos and slogans, by the style and "look" of their advertising, and by the kind of copy found in their advertisements. Differentiation is a crucial element in branding, for what brands celebrate is not only what is distinctive about their products but also how they differ from their competitors.

Digital

Peter Lunenfeld, who has written a number of books on art and the new technologies, explains what the term "digital" means in his book, *The Digital Dialectic: New Essays on New Media*. He writes (1999, Cambridge, MA: MIT Press, p. xv):

> Digital systems do not use continuously variable representational relationships. Instead, they translate all input into binary structures of Os and Is, which can then be stored, transferred, or manipulated at the level of numbers or "digits" (so called because etymologically, the word descends from the digits on our hand with which we count out those numbers). Thus a phone call on a digital system will be encoded as a series of these Os and Is and sent over the wires as binary information to be reinterpreted as speech on the other end....It is the capacity of the electronic computer to encode a vast variety of information digitally that has given it such a central place within contemporary culture. As all manner of representational systems are recast as digital information, then all can be stored, accessed, and controlled by the same equipment.

It is safe to say that the digital revolution has had a major impact on every aspect of life in contemporary society, from computers and digital television sets to smart phones and the internet. We live in a digital age, which has led to remarkable new developments in many areas of life.

Digital Campaign

With the development of social media such as Facebook and Twitter, advertising agencies now spend a great deal of time and energy on these media. A "digital campaign," then, would be a campaign focusing on using social media and other aspects of our digital culture, such as smartphones and tablets. An article by Todd Wasserman reveals that:

> global *digital advertising* spending broke $100 billion for the first time, according to eMarketer, which predicts the business will grow another 15.1% this year. That figure compares to a market increase of 17.8% in 2012. The slowing growth rate appears to be a natural consequence of the maturation of the industry— the larger it gets, the harder it is to grow. While figures for the entire ad industry's growth in 2012 aren't in yet, Magna Global last June predicted that the ad business would expand *4.8% worldwide* in 2012.
>
> Digital advertising's stronger growth means it's taking up more of the overall business. eMarketer estimates that online advertising accounted for just under 20% of all advertising. This year, 21.7% of the advertising pie will be taken up by digital advertising. The double-digit growth is expected to decline steadily until 2016. (mashable.com/2013/01/09/ digital-advertising-100-billion/)

Wasserman's statistics show that digital advertising is now a major component of the advertising industry, and accounts for 20 percent of all advertising expenditures.

Direct Address Advertising

This kind of advertising targets consumers directly and without an intermediary, by using email or snail mail to establish direct contact with potential consumers. If you're going to send an email or a letter to thousands of people or hundreds of thousands of people, it makes sense to use copywriters with expertise in this kind of selling. Direct address advertising targets individuals and corporations, in contrast to advertising that uses radio or television or other means directed towards audiences in general.

Direct Response Marketing

Direct response marketing uses advertising to elicit an immediate response from target audiences. Thus, direct response advertising makes it easy for potential consumers to act upon their preferences by doing things like offering toll-free telephone numbers, by offering email addresses or websites that can be clicked on to obtain more information or purchase the product, and by adding free "giveaways," little things like booklets or "webinars" to get potential customers to respond in a desired way.

Disposable Income

This is money that doesn't have to be saved for necessities like buying food or paying the mortgage. Collectively speaking, teenagers in America have a great deal of "disposable income," which they spend on clothes, music, movies, food, electronic gizmos, and other things. According to a Rand Youth Poll conducted September 8, 2012, we find:

25.6 million teens in the U.S.

208.7 billion dollars in spending (products bought by and for teens)

91.1 billion dollars annual teen income

$4,023 average annual income of 15- to 17-year-olds

21% percentage of teens who describe themselves as unemployed

(www.statisticbrain.com/teenage-consumer-spending-statistics/)

These figures indicate that teens have around $80 a week in income, most of which, we can assume, is disposable. Because of the economic difficulties the United States has faced in recent years, teen spending is actually down from what it was in 2000, when they spent an average of around $100 per week.

Douglas, Mary (England, 1921–2007)

Mary Douglas was an English social anthropologist who did work on cultures, what she called "natural" symbols, consumer cultures, and various aspects of social life. Many of the theories described in this book deal with personal decision-making as an important focus of advertising. In theory, when people shop for something, their decision to purchase that product is tied to their personalities and psychological makeup.

Mary Douglas argued that it is our group affiliations, not our personalities, that shape our shopping behavior. She developed what is called Grid-Group Theory to explain her position. Grid-Group Theory argues that everyone faces two problems: who am I (identity) and what should I do (behavior). "Group" deals with the strength of boundaries in the groups to which we belong, and "Grid" refers to the number and strengths of the rules in the group. These two dimensions lead to four lifestyles:

Boundaries	Number and Kind of Rules	Lifestyle
Strong	Numerous and varied	Elitists
Strong	Few	Egalitarians
Weak	Few	Individualists
Weak	Numerous and varied	Fatalists

We rarely recognize that we belong to one of these lifestyles, but our behavior in many different realms is shaped by messages we pick up, at the unconscious level, from the lifestyle to which we have become attached, even though we are unaware of doing so.

Douglas turns her attention to shopping, which she explains from a Grid-Group perspective. She writes, in an article titled "In Defence of Shopping" (in P. Falk and C. Campbell, Eds., 1997, *The Shopping Experience*, Sage: London, pp. 17–18):

We have to make a radical shift away from thinking about consumption as a manifestation of individual choices. Culture itself is the result of myriads of individual choices, not primarily between commodities but between kinds of relationships. The basic choice that a rational individual has to make is the choice about what kind of society to live in. According to that choice, the rest follows. Artefacts are selected to demonstrate the choice. Food is eaten, clothes are worn, cinema, books, music, holidays, all the rest are choices that conform with the initial choice for a form of society.

If Douglas is correct, it is the choice we unconsciously make about a lifestyle to identify with that most directly shapes our behavior as consumers. If this is so, then advertisers must focus on group beliefs and affiliations rather than personal taste.

Emoticons

Emoticons originally developed as people used characters on their keyboards to express certain emotions, such as ;-) for winking. Now many word processing programs provide drawings of emoticons for writers to use.

Extreme Close Up

An extreme close up has a powerful impact on viewers because it takes part of a human body, such as a woman's lips, and uses them to attract attention and perhaps generate emotions—most likely sexual turn-ons—in people exposed to them. The Chanel advertisement is an extreme close up of a woman's lips and has a powerful impact that is based on the sexual nature of human lips. What this advertisement does, it would seem, is to excite us and teach us to connect the Chanel brand with sexuality in our unconscious.

This advertisement for Chanel lipstick uses an extreme close up that shows only the model's lips—and not even all of her lips. Lips are tactile sensory organs that play a role in our sexual activities.

Facebook

Facebook is the largest social media site with more than one billion people using it. It allows people to attach images and video to messages members put on Facebook that are accessible to their followers.

Advertising on Facebook

Facebook makes most of its money through ads. Here's a quick example to show you how it works.

A Business Creates an Ad

Let's say a gym opens in your neighborhood. The owner creates an ad to get people to come in for a free workout.

Facebook Gets Paid To Deliver the Ad

The owner sends the ad to Facebook and describes who should see it: people who live nearby and like running.

The Right People See the Ad

Facebook shows you the ad if you live in town and like to run. That's how advertisers reach you without Facebook sharing your private info.

Ads Help Keep Facebook Free

From the beginning, the people who built Facebook wanted it to be free for everyone. It now costs over a billion dollars a year to run Facebook, and delivering ads is how Facebook pays for this.

You See Personalized Ads

Facebook tries to show you the ads you'll be most interested in. These ads are chosen based on the things you do with

Facebook, such as liking a page, and info Facebook receives from you and other sources.

You Can Impact the Ads You See

Unlike ads on television, you can influence which ads you see on Facebook. Spot something that doesn't interest you? Click the X and it's gone.

Facebook is now in the process of figuring out how to make money from the billion people who use it without offending them. An audience of one billion people is extremely tempting to advertisers, since certain members of Facebook can be targeted for ads of interest to them. And Facebook knows a great deal about everyone who uses it. Recently, it introduced an internal search program which enables members of Facebook to find other members with similar tastes and interests—a matter of considerable value to advertising agencies.

Fads

Fads can be described as suddenly popular styles of hair, clothes, dances, foods, or anything else that is adopted by a large number of people, generally for a short period of time—that is, until the next fad becomes popular.

Feminist Theory

Feminist theorists have argued for many years about the way advertising exploits the female body to sell products and services. For feminists, advertising plays a particularly important role in giving women simplistic and absurd notions about what it is to be a woman, about women's status and their possibilities. The fact that so many women adopt the views of advertising agencies and acquiesce to their sexploitation is particularly upsetting to feminist theorists. In recent years, advertising agencies have taken to showing only parts of women's bodies, as in the advertisement depicted here, de-emphasizing women as human beings and stressing only parts of their bodies, generally sexual in nature, of use in selling products.

This advertisement for Le Mystere is unusual in that it combines both a glimpse of the model's breast and of the cleavage in her buttocks—the two most erogenous areas in a woman's body. It is an example of the kind of sexploitation of women that both male and female Feminists deplore.

Focal Points in the Study of Advertising

When examining advertising and mediated communication of any kind, there are, I would suggest, five focal points to consider:

Artists: create advertisements and commercials (writers, actors, musicians, etc.)

Audiences: people who listen to, read, or watch the advertisements

America: the country where the advertisements are made

Ads: the commercials or print advertisements

Media: which convey print ads and commercials to the audience

This chart below shows their possible relationships:

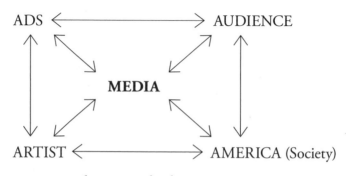

Focal Points and Advertising

Depending upon our interests, we can examine the relationship that exists between ads and the artists and copywriters who create them, ads and the audience that reads or watches them, ads and American society, ads and the media in which they are found, or any other combination of the focal points. The growth of advertising on the internet and in social media has been the most important recent development in the advertising industry. I discuss this phenomenon in a number of different places in this dictionary.

Focus Groups

Many advertising agencies run focus groups in which they bring together a small group of people, usually eight to ten, and a moderator. The agencies try to obtain information about how members of the focus group feel about products, print ads, commercials, and anything else that they can use in their advertising. If the focus group is not representative of the target audience for the product being advertised or is dominated by one or two people, the material obtained from the group may not be useful. In addition, focus groups generally don't get into the deeper meanings that products have for people, so some marketing theorists, such as Gerald Zaltman at the Harvard Business School, suggest that intensive interviews with one or two people are more useful than focus groups.

Freud, Sigmund (Moravia, 1856–1939)

Sigmund Freud, the father of modern psychoanalysis, was the most influential psychologist of his era and one of the most important thinkers of the twentieth century. He was trained as physician at the University of Vienna, but became interested in the human psyche after reading Dostoevsky, Nietzsche, and other authors. He established a practice in Vienna to treat patients with nervous diseases and over the years developed his theories about psychoanalysis that he expounded in books such as *The Interpretation of Dreams* (1900), *The Psychopathology of Everyday Life* (1901), *Civilization and Its Discontents* (1929), and his pioneering study of humor, *Jokes and Their Relation to the Unconscious* (1905).

Freudian Perspectives on How Advertising Works

One of Freud's main contributions to psychoanalytic theory was his explanation of the different levels of the human psyche. For Freud, the psyche is like an iceberg. The part of the iceberg we see above the water is what we are conscious of. For a few feet below the water we can still make out, dimly, the iceberg and what he called the subconscious. And then, buried in darkness and representing most of our psyches, is the unconscious. Freud wrote (1963, *Freud: Character and Culture,* Phillip Rief, Ed., New York: Collier Books, p. 189), "What is in your mind is not identical with what you are conscious of; whether something is going on in your mind and whether you hear of it are two different things." In other words, we are not aware of much that is in our minds—especially material lodged in our unconscious.

CONSCIOUS

SUBCONSCIOUS

UNCONSCIOUS

Although we are unable to access our unconscious, without the assistance of a depth psychologist or psychoanalyst, material buried in it shapes our behavior. As Gerald Zaltman, a marketing professor at the Harvard Business School, explains in his book, *How Customers Think: Essential Insights into the Mind of the Market* (2003, Boston: Harvard Business School Press, pp. 8–9), consumers mistakenly believe:

> that most of our thinking occurs in our conscious minds. In actuality consumers have far less access to their own mental activities than marketers give them credit for. Ninety-five percent of our thinking takes place in our unconscious minds—that wonderful, if messy, stew of memories, emotions, thoughts and other cognitive processes we're not aware of or that we can't articulate.

He adds that in our minds, our emotional system usually dominates our logical system, or, as he writes, "typically exerts the *first* force on our thinking and behavior." We may think we are rational, but if Zaltman is correct, it is our emotions that affect and shape our behavior. We are more rationalizers than rational beings.

Freud had a second theory about the psyche. He suggested that there are three competing forces in our psyches:

The ID: desire, lust, and the wish for immediate gratifications

The EGO: survival and maintaining equilibrium in the psyche

The SUPEREGO: guilt and conscience

Advertising works by appealing to Id elements in our psyche by stimulating desire and neutralizing, to the extent it can, the Superego and Ego elements in our psyches. This theory is known as Freud's "structural" hypothesis, and it came after his "topographic" hypothesis, which deals with the three layers of the mind. Many culture theorists adapt psychoanalytic thought in their analyses of particular advertisements, commercials, and advertising in general.

Advertising now has extended its reach, and uses "product placements" to put certain products in television shows and films as a means of reaching people, has advertisements on cell phones, and advertising on the internet. In some cases, a product placement in a television show or film can lead to significant increases in the sales of that product. It is now the case, that, with few exceptions, wherever in the world there are flat surfaces, such as screens of all kinds and sizes, from cell phones to television sets, and the sides of buildings, cars, and buses, advertisers will find a way to exploit them for their purposes. Because we envy celebrities and movie stars and want to imitate their behavior, product placements are often very successful.

G

Gender

The way women are portrayed in advertising is a subject that has interested social scientists for many years. Sociologist Erving Goffman's *Gender Advertisements,* published in 1976, found that women are generally portrayed in advertisements as weaker and smaller than males and subservient to them. The exploitation of women's sexuality, known as "sexploitation," is also a major problem that feminist critics of the media complain about. Women are turned in many advertisements into little more than sexual objects whose bodies, breasts, and other sexually exciting features are exploited by advertisers. In many advertisements we do not see the whole woman, but only part of her—which suggests that women are not seen as persons but as beings with certain body parts of particular interest to men.

Global Marketing

Marketing is now a global phenomenon, and advertising agencies are increasingly part of large international advertising organizations that can accommodate the desires of corporations to mount campaigns and reach people in many different countries. Many brands are now worldwide and wish to use international advertising agencies with a global reach. These global agencies can have agencies in each country mount a campaign that reflects the values and beliefs of people in that country.

Guerilla Marketing

This kind of advertising uses unconventional and inexpensive methods to sell products and services. The term comes from Jay Levinson's 1983 book, *Guerrilla Marketing: Easy and Inexpensive Strategies for Making Big Profits from Your Small Business* (Boston: Houghton-Mifflin). The metaphor suggests "guerilla" warfare in which a group is overmatched against traditional opponents but manages to succeed somehow.

Hard Sell and Soft Sell

Advertising agencies distinguish between what they call a "hard sell" and a "soft sell." A hard sell is one in which the advertisements and commercials are very direct in their attempts to sell the product. They focus on its features and pressure viewers to purchase the product, often making it possible to do so immediately by calling a telephone number or clicking on something in an internet advertisement. "Buy now" is the mantra. This is quite different from a "soft sell" in which there is no pressure in the advertisement or commercial to act immediately.

"Soft sell" advertisements attempt to create a certain feeling in people exposed to them that eventually will lead to sales. The advertisements often have strong entertainment qualities which build a feeling of goodwill towards the product being advertised that will eventually pay off for the advertisers.

Humor

Many advertisements and commercials use humor because people obtain pleasure from the humor (when it is successful), and that feeling of pleasure or happiness is transferred, advertisers hope, to whatever they are trying to sell. Surveys reveal that a large percentage of the American public feels that ads and commercials are intrusive and are irritated by them. If a text amuses and entertains audiences, that may help keep them be attentive to the text. Some people in advertising feel that humor has certain negative aspects in that it distracts audiences exposed to the advertising from the selling message. In addition, some people may not "get" the humor or may be antagonized by it. So humor is dangerous, but when it works, it can be very effective as a selling tool.

I

Icons

In semiotic theory, an icon is something that conveys meaning by resembling something else. C. S. Peirce had a trichotomy involving three ways that meaning is generated: by icons (resemblance), indexes (cause and effect), and symbols (must be learned). In recent years, the term "iconic" has become very popular and is used to describe something or someone that is extraordinary or exemplary. A product that has become "iconic" is one that has achieved widespread attention and notoriety. Some "iconic" products would be the Apple iPhone, Levi's jeans, Coca-Cola, and the "Big Mac." You can find lists of other iconic products on Google, itself an icon.

Ideologies in Advertising

The main point that Marxists like Henri Lefebvre and John Berger, who are discussed in this book, make is that advertising is not just an irritation but an important institution in bourgeois capitalist societies. It is the duty of Marxists to search out the hidden ideologies found in particular advertisements and commercials and expose them. This process, they hope, will weaken the power of the "unmasked" advertisement to support capitalism and a political system that is destructive of the well-being of the average man and woman.

Image

Images are all pervasive. We swim in a sea of images from the moment we wake up until we go to sleep, but even when we are asleep, according to Freud, we dream in images that we patch together and call dreams. Images have great power. The images of the twin towers crumbling in New York were full of meaning for everyone who saw them and led to profound changes in the way Americans thought about our country and our susceptibility to terrorist attacks.

Semiotically speaking, an image is a collection of signs, each of which helps convey meaning to us when we look at it. And those signs often have signs within them. Thus, a glass of champagne is a sign that conveys certain meanings to us—suggesting happiness, celebrations, and events of importance—which we learn by convention. But within that champagne are small bubbles, which are also signs. So there are often signs inside of signs.

In this image of a blonde woman racing through a building with a sledge-hammer, we have, aside from her role in the commercial, an intertextual connection to the Biblical story of David and Goliath.

In the Macintosh "1984" commercial, there are images of a blonde woman running and holding a sledgehammer. We can read and understand this image on four different levels:

Literal Level: What we see in the image
Textual Level: Where the image fits in the text
Intertextual Level: Similar images called to mind from other texts
Mythic Level: The relation of the image to cultural myths and legends

What I call the "mythic level" is really part of the intertextual level, but since myths have so much resonance in cultures, I gave the mythic level emphasis.

There are many ways that images convey meaning. Sometimes they work by making us recall information we already know and striking responsive chords in our minds. There is a theory of communication, the "responsive chord theory," which argues that the communication process relies, to a great degree, on information people already know, and thus, what communication does, in effect, is to strike responsive chords using the material stored in our minds. Sometime we recognize that an image is similar to other images we've seen and thus have an intertextual connection with. In addition, sometimes an image makes us recall some myth which helps give the image a deeper meaning. This process may function at the unconscious level, but that doesn't mean we aren't affected by the images. Freud said dreams are the royal road to the unconscious. When thinking about advertisements and commercials, we can say *images* are the royal road to the unconscious—and it is the unconscious that shapes much of our behavior and many of our purchasing decisions.

Image Advertising

Image advertising involves creating images of a product in a consumer's mind that generate the feelings, attitudes, and beliefs the consumer has about a product. This image is based on cues a brand's advertising offers about the status, qualities, and attributes of the product.

Imprinting

Imprinting refers to the process, described by Clotaire Rapaille, by which young children learn the basic codes in the countries where they are raised. It takes place, he suggests, during the first seven years of their lives and shapes their behavior as consumers and in many other ways as well. Advertisers in every country seek to identify and use these imprints, which reflect core values, for their purposes.

Infomercial

Infomercials are wolves in sheep's clothing. They typically are thirty- or sixty-minute television programs that can be thought of as extended commercials created to sell some product by demonstrating what it can do. They are not usually offered during prime-time television. Strange as it might seem, many people like watching infomercials, and these extended commercials have had some remarkable successes. A Salton-Maxim Juiceman infomercial sold 52 million dollars worth of the Juicemen in one night. Infomercials often have direct-response facets to them, with toll free telephone numbers.

Information Overload

The term "information overload" was popularized by futurist Alvin Toffler in his book, *Future Shock,* in 1970. It involves a kind of numbness and inability to think clearly and function effectively because we have too much information to process it correctly. It is relevant to advertising because it may occur when we are exposed to too many advertisements, what we can call "clutter," and end up not being able to remember any of them and differentiate between them.

Internet

The internet (also known as "the net," "the information superhighway," and "cyberspace") is a global system of interconnected computer networks that uses standard internet protocols to serve billions of people all over the world.

One can find everything on the internet, from jokes to instructions for making bombs. Thanks to the internet we can communicate with anyone anywhere, find partners to marry, and learn how to cook foods from every country. Much of the knowledge created over the centuries, from the ideas of Greek philosophers to news about current events, is now available on the internet. Blue Onion, an advertising agency (www.digourideas.com), defines the internet in its glossary as:

a worldwide network of networks that all use the TCP/IP communications protocol and share a common address space. First incarnated as the ARPANET in 1969, the Internet has metamorphosed from a military internetwork to an academic research internetwork to the current commercial internetwork. It commonly supports services such as email, the World Wide Web, file transfer, and Internet Relay Chat. The Internet is experiencing tremendous growth in the number of users, hosts, and domain names. It is gradually subsuming other media, such as proprietary computer networks, newspapers, books, television, and the telephone.

Intertextuality

This concept refers to the notion that films, television shows, novels, advertisements, and other kinds of texts always borrow, sometimes unconsciously, from other texts that preceded them. The concept comes from the work of a Russian theorist, M. M. Bakhtin. He said that language is "dialogic," in that when we speak, what we say is tied to the past—to things that have been said before, and to the future—statements that we expect to be made in the future. His theory applies not only to the spoken word but to literary texts, films, television shows, and all kinds of other art forms, including advertising. As he explains in his book, *The Dialogic Imagination: Four Essays* (1981, Austin: University of Texas Press, p. 280):

> The word in living conversation is directly, blatantly, oriented toward a future answer-word: it provokes an answer, anticipates it and structures itself on the answer's direction. Forming itself in an atmosphere of the already spoken, the word is at the same time determined by that which has not yet been said but which is needed and in fact anticipated by the answering word. Such is the situation in any living dialogue.

When we apply this theory to texts, we can understand what intertextuality is. Intertextuality asserts that all texts borrow from texts created in the past and that, according to some theorists, all texts are made up of borrowed material—sometimes the borrowing is consciously done, but most of the time it is not. Bakhtin calls this borrowing between texts "quotations," and we now call this borrowing intertextuality.

A good example of intertextuality can be found in the famous "1984" Macintosh commercial by Ridley Scott. The use of "1984" immediately calls to mind George Orwell's dystopian novel, *1984,* but there is also a scene in which a beautiful blonde woman throws a sledgehammer at a gigantic television screen and destroys it. On the screen a representative of the rulers of the institution in which the skinheads are confined is talking gibberish to them. The woman throws the sledgehammer, and it destroys the image. This scene can be seen as a modernization of the David and Goliath tale in the Bible, in which David slings a stone and kills the giant Goliath. What it suggests is that advertisers can use intertextual references— information members of audiences have in their heads, in this case knowledge about the novel *1984* and about the story of David and Goliath—to give ads and commercials more resonance and power for those who recognize the intertextual references. This commercial achieves its power by its intertextual connection to the Bible; Apple also uses the story of Adam and Eve eating from the tree of knowledge in its logo. The bite out of the apple in the Apple logo informs us that Adam and Eve have eaten from the tree of knowledge and will be expelled from the Garden of Eden.

L

This is the Starbucks coffee logo, one of the most frequently encountered logos in our daily lives. Earlier Starbucks logos were more complicated and more difficult to read.

The red forward slash is the logo for TBWA\Worldwide, one of the major advertising agencies. Notice the simplicity of the logo, a minimalist image with a focus on the future. *Used with permission of TBWA.*

Logos

Logos are symbolic designs which organizations, corporations, and groups use to identify themselves. The Starbucks logo is one of the most familiar logos in the United States and in many other countries. It identifies Starbucks coffee houses and products. As styles change and companies wish to update their images, they do so by updating their logos. The Starbucks logo is the latest one in a series used by the company. Logos are used by brands to give their products and services an identity and to say something about the company that uses them. The TWBA logo is extremely simple—a forward slash, that requires the viewer to imagine what it signifies. TWBA offers an analysis of its logo, which concludes as follows:

It is a symbol of our prime skills.

Our ability to see and define the possibilities of tomorrow,

And to transform a client's future through the power of an idea.

It is our diagonal lightening rod for change.

Lois, George (American, 1931–)

George Lois is one of the most celebrated (and controversial) art directors and designers in the advertising industry. He has won numerous awards in the course of his career and was honored with a show of his *Esquire Covers* in the Museum of Modern Art in New York City. His work can be seen at www.georgelois.com/ad_campaigns.html, where there is also a good deal of autobiographical material on his career and material on the numerous campaigns he ran for a wide variety of clients.

M

Madison Avenue

Madison Avenue is famous because it is the street on which many of the most prestigious advertising agencies in New York are located. Madison Avenue is now synonymous with advertising in American popular culture and provided the title for the popular television show, *Mad Men.*

Mad Men

George Lois is a celebrated art director whose comments about the popular television show, *Mad Men,* reflect the resentment that many art directors and copy writers in advertising agencies feel about the non-creative administrators in agencies, who often were in positions of power and could prevent graphic artists and copywriters from doing their best work. As Lois explained on CNN (March 24, 2012), *"TV 'Mad Men' real? I don't think so"*:

> *Mad Men* misrepresents the advertising industry of my time by ignoring the dynamics of the Creative Revolution that changed

the world of communications forever....That dynamic period of counterculture in the 1960s found expression on Madison Avenue through a new creative generation—a rebellious coterie of art directors and *copywriters* who understood that visual and verbal expression were indivisible, who bridled under the old rules that consigned them to secondary roles in the ad-making process dominated by non-creative hacks and technocrats....It was a testy time to be a graphic designer like me who had the rage to communicate and to create icon rather than con. And, unlike the TV *Mad Men*, we worked full, exhausting, joyous days: pitching *new business*, creating ideas, "comping" them up, storyboarding them, selling them, photographing them, and directing commercials. (www.cnn.com/2012/03/24/opinion/lois-mad-men)

Advertising is a "glamour" industry, and people who work in the top agencies often make a great deal of money—but they also work very hard and live in a constant state of tension, because at any moment one of their major clients that is spending millions or hundreds of millions of dollars on a campaign can decide to find another agency—which means that fifty to a hundred employees of the agency might be fired, unless the agency lands another client with a large advertising budget very quickly.

Manipulation

The notion that advertising "manipulates" people was once popular with Marxist critics, but has been abandoned in recent years because, so these critics argue, all media manipulate people. As Hans Magnus Enzenberger, a German poet and media theorist, writes in *The Consciousness Industry: On Literature, Politics & the Media* (1974, New York: Seabury, p. 104):

Manipulation—etymologically, "handling," means technical treatment of a given material with a particular goal in mind. When the technical intervention is of immediate social relevance, then manipulation is a political act. In the case of the media industry, that is by definition the case.

Thus every use of the media presupposes manipulation. The most elementary processes in media production, from the choice of the medium itself to shooting, cutting, synchronization, dubbing right up to distribution, are all operations carried out on raw material. There is no such thing as unmanipulated writing, filming or broadcasting. The question is therefore not whether the media are manipulated, but who manipulates them. A revolutionary plan should not require the manipulators to disappear; on the contrary, it must make everyone a manipulator.

One can only wonder what Enzenberger would think about the contemporary digital world in which so many people create media and are, in his terms, "democratic" manipulators.

Enzenberger starts his book with an essay on what he describes as "The Industrialization of the Mind." He writes (p. 3):

All of us, no matter how irresolute we are, like to think that we reign supreme in our own consciousness, that we are masters of what our minds accept or reject....No illusion is more stubbornly upheld than the sovereignty of the mind. It is a good example of the impact of philosophy on people who ignore it; for the idea that men can "make up their minds" individually and by themselves is essentially derived from the tenets of bourgeois philosophy.... We might do worse, I think, than dust off the admirably laconic statement which one of our classics made more than a century ago: "What is going on in our minds has always been, and will always be, a product of society."

The quote that ends this passage is from Karl Marx. The thrust of Enzenberger's thought, in the two selections of I have quoted, is that we are under illusions if we think that we can "make up our minds" and that we are the sovereign rulers of our minds. No, it is the people within the media who manipulate images and sounds and other things that play a major role in shaping our thoughts and behavior—and, of particular importance, our consumption patterns. Television, radio, the cinema, fashion, design, and advertising are, he argues, all part of "the mind industry," and it is this industry whose main purpose is not so much to sell products as to sell the existing political order. With advertising and many of the other arts mentioned above we have the ironic situation of creative and avant-garde techniques used to prop up "the prevailing pattern of man's domination by man" (p. 10).

Marketing

Marketing, broadly speaking, involves the process of selling products and services to people and uses advertising as the means to accomplish this goal. Some theorists of marketing have a very broad understanding of the term and see it as involving everything from the corporate culture of the company manufacturing a product to the way a product is sold by advertising agencies. The narrow view of marketing sees it as a means of writing messages on the so-called blank slate minds of consumers and assumes that if advertising agencies can find the right words or catchy slogan, they can sell the product. The broader view of marketing is that one must consider the culture in which a product is being created and sold and the complex relationship that exists between consumers and producers.

Marketers are famous for breaking societies down into various segments or groupings, such as the Claritas 66 groupings of American society or the Stanford Research Institute's Values and Lifestyle (VAL) typology developed in the seventies. In theory, the members of one of these groupings are susceptible to advertising directed toward them and their values. The first VALS typology broke American society into groups such as survivors, sustainers, belongers, emulators, achievers, I-am-Me's, experientials, and societally conscious individuals.

Because marketers seldom can find causal relationships between advertising campaigns and the behavior of consumers, they rely on correlations. If an advertising campaign leads to a major upturn in the sales of a client, they can assume that the campaign has a positive impact. But did the campaign convince an individual to buy the product being advertised, or did it send messages to the lifestyle group to which the individual belongs and which sends subtle messages about what to consume?

Marketing Mix (also known as The Four P's)

The "marketing mix" covers the basic elements to be considered in marketing a product, each of which starts with the letter "P," so these elements are often called "The Four P's." The mix is described as follows at 4marketingps.blogspot.com/2009/09/4-marketing-ps.html:

> **Product** The product aspects of marketing deal with the specifications of the actual goods or services, plus how it relates to the end users needs and wants. The range of a product normally includes supporting elements such as warranties, guarantees, and support.

> **Pricing** This refers to the process of setting a price for a product, together with discounts. The price need not be monetary; it can plainly be what is exchanged for the product or services, e.g. time, energy, or attention. Methods of setting prices optimally are in the domain of pricing art.

> **Placement** (or distribution): refers to how the product gets to the buyer; for instance, point-of-sale assignment or retailing. This third P has furthermore at times been called Place, referring to the channel by which a product or service is sold (e.g. online vs. retail), which geographic region or industry, to which division (young adults, families, business citizens), etc., also referring to how the surroundings in which the product is sold...can influence sales.

> **Promotion** This includes advertising, sales promotion, including promotional education, publicity, and individual selling. Branding refers to the assorted strategies of promoting the product, brand, or company.

The marketing mix, which has been around since the 1960s, alerts marketers to matters they must consider when planning a campaign. These topics are discussed in various places in this book.

Marx, Karl (Germany, 1818–1883)

Marx was one of the most influential thinkers of the nineteenth century, whose ideas and writings have shaped the thinking of many social scientists, writers, and scholars interested in culture and society. Among his writings are *The German Ideology* (with Friedrich Engels, 1845) and *A Contribution to the Critique of Political Economy* (1859).

Marxists on How Advertising Works

For Marxists, advertising plays a major role in capitalism and helps shape our consciousness and our behavior—leading to materialism and consumer cultures, in which private expenditures are stressed more than public investment for the general welfare in areas such as education, health, and building the infrastructure. I discussed Marx's notion of alienation when I defined that term, since it is central to the Marxist critique of capitalism.

Henri Lefebvre, a French Marxist, explains one aspect of advertising in his book, *Everyday Life in the Modern World* (1971, New Brunswick, NJ: Transaction, p. 105):

> In the second half of the twentieth century in Europe, or at any rate in France, there is nothing—whether object, individual, or social group—that is valued apart from its double, the image that advertises and sanctifies it. This image duplicates not only an object's material, perceptible existence but desire and pleasure that it makes into fictions situating them in the land of make-believe, promising "happiness"—the happiness of being a consumer. Thus publicity [advertising] that was intended to promote consumption is the first of consumer goods; it creates myths—or since it can create nothing—it borrows existing

myths, canalizing signifiers to a dual purpose: to offer them as such for general consumption and to stimulate the consumption of a specific object.

Lefebvre and many others scholars seek to explain to people the role advertising plays in their lives and in their societies. For them, advertising is not just a nuisance but one of the most important institutions of modern capitalist society and plays a major role in maintaining capitalism and the political order.

In the third edition of *Social Communication in Advertising: Consumption in the Mediated Marketplace*, William Leiss, Stephen Kline, Sut Jhally, and Jacqueline Botterill explain why advertising is so important. They write (2005, New York: Routledge, pp. 244–245):

> In the consumer society, we maintain, no institutions are more directly concerned with providing patterned systems of meaning for consumption activity than marketing and advertising.... Advertising should be understood as a major cultural institution, not merely just another of businesses' tax-deductible expenditures, because the world of goods that composes the manifest or surface level of its productions is itself one of the principle channels of social communication.

This explains why advertising is such an interesting topic to analyze—because it is more than a means of selling goods and services; it shapes our cultures and society and, in so doing, affects in various ways individuals who live in these societies and cultures.

Maslow, Abraham (American, 1908–1970)

Abraham Maslow was an American psychologist celebrated for his "theory of needs," which is discussed next. He held professorships at institutions such as Brandeis University, the New School for Social Research, and Columbia University.

Maslow's Theory of Needs

Abraham Maslow was a psychologist who developed a very influential theory about human needs that can be applied to advertising. In his book, *Shoptimism,* Lee Eisenberg describes Maslow's work on needs (2009, New York: Free Press, p. 82):

> In 1943, when he was in his midthirties, Abraham Maslow outlined how our behavior is driven by the quest to satisfy a series of needs. Once we address what Maslow called…"lower-order needs" we move on to ascending "higher order needs." Some of these needs can be more material than others, meaning that the Buy comes into play as a means to satisfy them. Our need for safety and security is first, followed by our need to belong—our need for love and friendship and all that. Then there's our need for self-respect and dignity. And finally there's our need to "self-actualize," to realize our full, individual potential.

In the chart below we start with higher order needs at the top and move to lower order needs as we descend to the bottom.

Self-Actualization Needs
Esteem Needs (status, prestige, recognition)
Social Needs (group membership, community, belonging)
Safety Needs (physical safety, economic security)
Physical Survival Needs (food, health, material goods, safety)

For Maslow, the American Dream basically involved lower order needs such as our desire for material goods. At the highest level, we realize our potential and live self-actualized lives. Maslow's theory, writes Kalman Applbaum in *The Marketing Era: From Professional Practice to Global Provisioning,* "was often referred to me and appeared to be the most prevalent, hallowed, and fertile behavioral theory behind marketing practice" (2004, New York: Routledge, p. 99). The reason why Maslow's theory is so popular is that it deals with the needs of normal people, not disturbed ones, and helps explain why people behave the way they do—a subject of obvious interest to advertising and marketing professionals and one that continues to confound them.

Material Culture

"Material culture" is the term used in the social sciences for relatively simple objects showing human workmanship. A screwdriver is an example of material culture. A battleship is not and neither is a car. They are complex mechanisms and are full of smaller objects that are part of material culture. Most of the things we buy are part of material culture—our clothes, our fragrances, our eyeglasses and sunglasses, our watches, and so on ad infinitum. Anthropologists study material culture because it contains information about the level of technical development in a culture and about the lifestyle of the people in that culture.

We can also say that the things we buy reflect us and send messages to others about what we are like, what we can afford, how sophisticated our taste is, our political leanings, and many other matters. Advertisers often say "You are what you buy." What this means is that our purchases reflect our personalities and taste. But what about people who buy things "above" them and are poseurs, making claims with their purchases to a higher status than they actually have? Some sociologists adopt a theatrical metaphor to social life and suggest that we see the world as a stage, our behavior can be seen as a kind of acting, and the things we buy can be seen as props that are designed to shape the opinions of others about us.

Materialism

The materialism I'm concerned with here doesn't directly involve Marx's philosophical materialism, his materialist theory of history, and his notion that the economic base shapes the cultural superstructure in capitalist societies and their dominant institutions. Materialism, as I understand the term, is mostly psychological in nature and refers to an all-powerful desire, perhaps "passion" is a better word, found in many people to buy things that will satisfy their desires for the "good things in life" and reinforce their sense of achievement.

This focus on obtaining material goods is privatistic and, as we shall see, religious in nature, in that the focus is on individuals buying what they desire and not on spending money in public investment for the general welfare. This attitude can be connected to capitalism and to the role advertising plays in first world capitalist societies.

Max Weber, one of the greatest sociological theorists of the twentieth century, suggested that Calvinism, or what he called "the Protestant ethic," led to the development of capitalism. His book, *The Protestant Ethic and the Spirit of Capitalism,* focuses on the impact of the Protestant ethic on modern societies and its role in the development of materialism and capitalism. The Protestant ethic loosened the grip on people's minds of medieval notions about the value of poverty and, at the same time, justified consumption as something that God wants people to do, something that has a divine significance. And that consumption requires money.

Protestant thought argued, Weber explained, that there is a "Divine Providence" which explains the unequal distribution of wealth. This was a great comfort to wealthy people for it justified their position. It also suggests that efforts to help the poor are fruitless, since such efforts are against Divine Providence. At the conclusion of his book, Weber discusses the ideas of a Puritan minister, Richard Baxter, who believed that "the care for external goods should only lie on the shoulders of the 'saint like a light cloak, which can be thrown aside at any moment.' But fate decreed that the cloak should become an iron cage" (1958, *The Protestant Ethic and the Spirit of Capitalism,* New York: Charles Scribner's and Sons, p. 181).

Weber explained the changes that took place over the centuries after the middle ages, where Catholic asceticism was dominant. Protestantism argued that God made the world for people to enjoy. The spirit of this asceticism has, he wrote, escaped from the cage, and "material goods have gained an increasing and finally an inexorable power over the lives of men as at no previous period in history" (p. 181). Weber's book was published in German in 1904 and 1905, so his analysis of capitalism and his critique of what we now describe as materialism and consumer culture are more than one hundred years old.

Weber adds a lament about the developments he described, suggesting also that it is in America that the pursuit of wealth has reached its highest development (p. 182):

> No one knows who will live in this cage in the future, or whether at the end of this tremendous development entirely new prophets will arise, or there will be a mechanized petrification, embellished with a sort of convulsive self-importance. For of the last state of this cultural development, it might be truly said: "Specialists without spirit, sensualists without heart; this nullity imagines that it has attained a level of civilization never before achieved."

He concludes, on the last page of his book, as one might expect in a book titled *The Protestant Ethic and the Spirit of Capitalism,* that it is important to give religious ideas "a significance for culture and national character which they deserve."

Maximizers and Satisfizers

A psychologist named Barry Schwartz wrote a book, *The Paradox of Choice* (2003), that discussed his research into consumption patterns. He concluded that there were two types of consumers: "maximizers" and "satisfizers." Maximizers are obsessed with getting the best price for a product, have very high expectations, and are anxiety-ridden about their purchases. Satisfizers are just the opposite: they have modest expectations, they don't obsess about getting the right price or the best product, and are not anxiety ridden. "Good enough" is fine for them. Obviously, advertising agencies would find it useful to know whether they have to appeal to maximizers or satisfizers.

McLuhan, Marshall (Canada, 1911–1980)

Marshall McLuhan was the author of a number of important books about communication. His two most important books, I believe, are *Understanding Media,* which I quote from elsewhere in this book, and his first book, *The Mechanical Bride: Folklore of Industrial Man,* published first in 1951. *The Mechanical Bride* has many short chapters that deal with topics such as the role that popular culture, the media, comic strips, and advertising play in shaping people's consciousness. Most of the book is devoted to advertisements that McLuhan mines for their social and cultural importance. I use his analysis of a Coca-Cola ad in *The Mechanical Bride* in my discussion of Coca-Cola advertising.

He explains his method of operation in the preface to the book (paperback edition in 1967, Boston: Beacon Press, p. v):

> Ours is the first age in which many thousands of the best-trained individual minds have made it a full-time business to get inside the collective public mind. To get inside in order to manipulate, exploit, control is the object now. And to generate heat not light is the intention. To keep everybody in the helpless state engendered by prolonged mental rutting is the effect of many ads and much entertainment alike....The present book likewise makes few attempts to attach the very considerable currents and pressures set up around us today by the mechanical agencies of the press, radio, movies, and advertising. It does attempt to set the reader at the center of the revolving picture created by these affairs where he may observe the action that is in progress and in which everybody is involved. From the analysis of that action, it is hoped, many individual strategies may suggest themselves.

McLuhan's goal is to waken people from the "collective dream" in which they find themselves by using the methods of literary theory to show how advertising agencies manipulate people and strive to obtain the effects they seek—shaping consumer taste and behavior.

There are many short (two or three pages long) chapters in the book. Each contains an image—usually of some advertisement—and some elliptical questions, meant to make his readers think about some topic. Then he offers his analysis, often written in a rather jazzy style, of the social, psychological, economic, and cultural significance of the images and language found in the advertisement. McLuhan developed this strategy—of focusing upon popular culture—as a way of interesting his students in the courses he taught.

Metaphor

Metaphor communicates by making *analogies*. For example, saying "My love is a rose" is a metaphor. Metaphors always use a form of the verb "to be." A weaker form of metaphor is simile, which uses "like" or "as" in making analogies. Thus, saying "My love is like a rose" is a simile. Metaphor is not just something found in literary works; in truth, metaphors play an important role in our thinking and conceptualizations. Metaphors can be visual, as in the Spider-Man costume. Advertising makes great use of metaphors and similes since they are powerful ways of generating emotions in people. When Miller describes itself as the "champagne" of bottled beers, it is using a metaphor, suggesting it is of equal value in beers as champagne—a highly valued kind of sparkling wine. Gerald Zaltman deals with the power of metaphors in his book, *How Customers Think* (2003, Boston: Harvard Business School Press, p. 78):

> By inviting consumers to use metaphors as they talk about a product or service, researchers bring consumers' unconscious thoughts and feelings to a level of awareness where both parties can explore them more openly together....Metaphors direct consumers' attention, influence their perceptions, enable them to make sense of what they encounter, and influence their decisions and actions.

Zaltman has a broad definition of metaphors and includes similes, analogies, proverbs and allegories—any form that expresses one thought or idea in terms of another. Making metaphor, he adds, is a "fundamental aspect of the mind."

Metonymy

Metonymy communicates by using *associations* and, like metaphor, is an important means of communication. A Rolls Royce is a metonym for something extremely expensive and of great quality. A weaker form of metonymy is "synecdoche," in which a part of something can be used to stand for the whole thing or, in reverse, the whole can be used to stand for a part of something. Thus, the Pentagon is a synecdoche for the American military establishment and the White House for the presidency. Metaphor and metonymy are basic to everyday communication and to advertising, which makes great use of them verbally and visually.

Motivation Research

Motivation research is usually based on in-depth interviews with people made by psychologists. It seeks to find the unconscious feelings people have about products that motivate them to purchase them. Ernest Dichter is the so-called "father of motivational research." He defined a motivation in *The Strategy of Desire* (New Brunswick, NJ: Transaction) as "a composite of factors which result in a specific action intended to change an existing situation into a future one" (2002, New Brunswick, NJ: Transaction, p. 37). That change would be, ultimately, in purchasing some product or engaging in some kind of behavior desired by the company or entity using motivational research.

In Leiss et al.'s *Social Communication in Advertising*, 3rd edition, Dichter's contribution is described as follows (2005, New York: Routledge, p. 144):

> Motivation research, or in-depth studies of consumers, elicited criticism both within and outside the industry, because it represented a way of thinking about the consumer that seemed to violate many people's sense of propriety. To Ernest Dichter,

the major advocate of motivation research, the criticism implied that advertising was seeking to exploit the consumer's presumed unconscious and often irrational attachments to particular things. In fact, it was a natural extension of the application of modern psychological theory and methods to advertising. Motivation research borrowed at least two premises from Freudian psychology: that people's real motives are hidden and that they can be elicited through conversation and free association.

Dichter was a psychologist, and his organization used nondirective depth interviews, conducted by psychologists, instead of what he considered to be a more superficial and less useful methodology—asking people questions about how they feel about a product.

Myth

The Greek work "mythos" means story. We find a useful definition of myth in Raphael Patai's *Myth and Modern Man* in which he describes myths as follows (1972, Englewood Cliffs, NJ: Prentice-Hall, p. 2):

> Myth…is a traditional religious charter, which operates by validating laws, customs, rites, institutions and beliefs, or explaining socio-cultural situations and natural phenomena, and taking the form of stories, believed to be true, about divine beings and heroes.…Myths are dramatic stories that form a sacred charter either authorizing the continuance of ancient institutions, customs, rites and beliefs in the area where they are current, or approving alterations.

Myths, he adds, play an important role in shaping social life since "myth not only validates or authorizes customs, rites, institutions, beliefs, and so forth, but frequently is directly responsible for creating them" (p. 2). Because of the emotional attachment we have to myths, advertisers can use allusions to myths or modernized versions of myths to great effect. The Macintosh "1984" commercial achieved part of its power from its use of the David and Goliath myth. There are a large number of Greek and Roman myths that

This is a mosaic of the myth of Odysseus, who has been tied to the mast of his ship by his sailors so he won't be lured to his death by sirens. We find the story in Homer's *The Odyssey*.

people in Western societies know which can be used in advertisements. I developed a "myth model" that shows how myths can be found in various aspects of our lives.

a myth is defined as a sacred narrative that validates cultural beliefs and practices

psychoanalytic reflections of the myth (when we can find them)

historical manifestations of the myth (when we can find them)

the myth in elite culture (operas, theatre, serious novels, etc.)

the myth in mass-mediated or popular culture (songs, advertisements, TV shows)

the myth in everyday life (when we can recognize it)

We can see this myth model at work with the story of David and Goliath found in the Bible and familiar to many people in the Western world and, to some degree, elsewhere.

Myth/Sacred Story	David and Goliath
Psychoanalytic Manifestation	Oedipus Complex Small figure kills big figure
Historical Experience	Apple versus IBM
Elite Culture	Statue of David by Michelangelo
Popular Culture	1984 Macintosh commercial
Everyday Life	Children playing with slingshots

This myth model explains how the famous Macintosh "1984" commercial can be connected to myths, and, in particular, the myth of David and Goliath, and this connection helps give the commercial is meaning.

Mythologies

In his book, *Mythologies,* the Marxist semiotician Roland Barthes deals with French everyday life and has articles on professional wrestling (which he analyzes as popular theater), margarine, soap powders, and various other seemingly banal topics. In his preface to the 1970 edition he writes (1970, New York: Hill and Wang, p. 9):

> This book has a double theoretical framework: on the one hand an ideological critique bearing on the language of so-called mass culture; on the other, a first attempt to analyze semiologically the mechanics of this language. I had just read Saussure and as a result acquired the conviction that by treating "collective representations" as sign-systems, one might hope to go further than the pious show of unmasking them and account *in detail*

for the mystification which transforms petit-bourgeois culture into a universal nature.

Barthes tells us that he has just read Saussure, who was one of the fathers of semiotics, and will be using semiotics to analyze various aspects of mass culture.

In an article in another publication, he analyzed an advertisement for Panzani Pasta and showed how the colors, the design, and other aspects of the advertisement suggested "Italian-ness" to French people who were exposed to the advertisement. Barthes has an article on advertising in a collection of his essays called *The Semiotic Challenge*. The article, "The Advertising Message," offers a semiotic analysis of advertising. He begins the article as follows (1988, New York: Hill and Wang, p. 161):

> All advertising is a message; it involves a source of utterance, which is the firm owning the product being launched (and praised), a point of reception, which is the public, and a channel of transmission, which is precisely what is called the support of advertising; and, since the science of messages is today a very current matter, we can try to apply to the advertising message a method of analysis which come to us (quite recently) from linguistics; to do this we must adopt a position *immanent* to the object we wish to study, *i.e.*, must deliberately abandon any observation relative to the emission or to the reception of the message, and place ourselves at the level of the message itself: semantically—that is, from the point of view of communication—how is an advertising text constituted (the question is also valid for the image, but it is much more difficult to answer)?

This passage, one long, 153 word sentence, is an example of Barthes's writing style, which is often quite idiosyncratic and uses neologisms, words that Barthes invents. He uses this passage to introduce semiotics, looking at advertisements as signifiers and analyzing what two advertisements he discusses, one for margarine and the other for ice cream, signify.

Discussing the language used in advertising, Barthes writes in the same essay (p. 165):

> The "good" advertising message is the one that condenses in itself the richest rhetoric and attains with precision (often a single word) the great oneiric themes of humanity...which defines poetry....The criteria of advertising language are those of poetry: rhetorical figures, metaphors, puns.

It is Barthes's ability to see important and interesting things in matters that seem, at first sight, trivial or mundane that made him so popular. He was, without doubt, one of the most important French thinkers of recent years—one whose work influenced scholars in many different fields everywhere.

N

Narratives

Narratives are stories and are important because many television commercials have a narrative structure, though it is usually highly abbreviated. Print advertisements can be seen as moments captured from narratives that the viewers of the advertisement have to create in their minds. That is, they must imagine some kind of backstory that explains what the characters in print advertisements are like and how they ended up shown the way they are in the advertisement. We must recognize that narratives are one of the main ways we learn about life and the world; they are not only simple entertainments.

In an article on "Narrative and Sociology" in the *Journal of Contemporary Ethnology,* Laurel Richardson writes (volume 19, 1990, p. 118):

Narrative is the primary way through which humans organize their experiences into temporally meaningful episodes.... Narrative is both a mode of reasoning *and* a mode of representation. People can "apprehend" the world narratively and people can "tell" about the world narratively. According to Jerome Bruner...narrative reasoning is one of the two basic and universal human cognition modes. The other mode is the logico-scientific.....The logico-scientific mode looks for universal truth conditions, whereas the narrative mode looks for particular connections between events. Explanation in the narrative mode is contextually embedded, whereas the logico-scientific explanation is extracted from spatial and temporal events. Both modes are "rational" ways of making meaning.

Narratives, then, play an important part in our lives and are one of the most important ways we make sense of the world. This power that narratives have applies, by extension, to what we learn from narratives that others create for us—in songs, in videos, in novels, in television shows, in films, and, in particular, in the many commercials and print advertisements to which we are exposed.

Michel de Certeau discusses the ubiquitous nature of narratives in *The Practice of Everyday Life* (1984, Berkeley: University of California Press, p. 186):

From morning to night, narrations constantly haunt streets and buildings. They articulate our existences by teaching us what they must be. They "cover the event," that is to say, they make our legends (legenda, what is to be read and said) out of it. Captured by the radio (the voice is the law) as soon as he awakens, the listener walks all day long through the forest of narrativities from journalism, advertising, and television narrativities that still find time, as he is getting ready for bed, to slip a few final messages under the portals of sleep. Even more than the God told about by the theologians of earlier days, these stories have a providential and predestining function: they organize in advance our work, our celebrations, and even our dreams.

One of the most important kinds of narratives, as far as this dictionary is concerned, is the television commercial. About a quarter of every hour on national television is devoted to commercials. If we watch four hours of television, which is the average for many households, that means we can watch around an hour of commercials. If each commercial is thirty seconds, we watch 120 commercials each day, and we are exposed to other commercials on radio and other advertisements on the internet, on our cell phones and smart phones, and in newspapers and magazines.

Neuromarketing

Neuromarketers are now using magnetic resonance machines to study the brains of people in an attempt to bypass our thought processes and work directly on our brains. *Neuromarketing: Understanding the "Buy Buttons" in Your Customer's Brain,* by Patrick Renevoise and Christophe Morin, discusses new developments in advertising. Their book, published in 2007 (Nashville: Thomas Nelson), suggests it will enable advertisers to use the latest information in brain research to help increase sales. Advertising people use the term "clutter" to describe the many advertisements and commercials we are exposed to during a typical day. One goal they have is to "cut through" the clutter. As we read on the back cover of Renevoise and Morin's book:

> People are flooded by an average of 10,000 sales messages every day. That makes selling tougher than ever before. So how do you cut through the clutter? Unveiling the latest brain research and revolutionary marketing practices, the authors…teach highly effective techniques to help you deliver powerful, unique and memorable presentations that will have a major, lasting impact on potential buyers.

Neuromarketing is just in its beginning stages, and the practitioners of neuromarketing haven't learned yet how to bypass our thought processes and get us to purchase products based on what the marketers have learned from watching sections of our brains light up when some product is mentioned to us. Neuromarketers haven't been able to do so yet, but they hope that some day in the not too distant future they will be able to use what they've learned from scanning our brains to shape our behavior as consumers.

Nonverbal Communication

It has been estimated that something like 70 percent of the communication we receive is non-verbal in nature, such as facial expressions, body language, and gestures that affect our emotions. If you look at television commercials, and turn off the sound, you will notice the way the actors and actresses in these texts use extreme facial expressions and body language to capture our attention, to establish an emotional connection with us, and (they hope) to convince us to purchase what is being advertised.

P

Pavlov, Ivan (Russia, 1849–1936)

Ivan Pavlov won the Nobel Prize for research in physiology in 1904. His ideas have been instrumental in many fields. He is most famous for his theory (see next definition) of conditioned reflexes based on his research carried out on dogs.

Pavlov's Theories Applied to Advertising

The Russian psychologist Pavlov had a theory that helps explain consumer behavior. He sounded a bell every time he fed some dogs, who then responded to the bell by salivating. Some advertisers believe that a kind of Pavlovian conditioning explains

For people everywhere, Coca-Cola is seen as an iconic signifier of modernity and the good life. It also is closely associated with American culture. In this advertisement, Coca-Cola is united with another American icon, Santa Claus, to intensify its message and its wholesome American-ness.

why consumers react to advertising the way they do. In an article by John Koten in *The Wall Street Journal,* an executive for Coca-Cola suggested that Pavlov should be considered the theorist who best explains how advertising works.

Do television commercials make people behave like Pavlov's dogs? Coca-Cola Co. says the answer is yes. In recent years the Atlanta soft-drink company has been refining an ad-testing procedure based on the behavioral principles developed by the Russian physiologist. So far, Coke says, its new testing system has worked remarkably well. In his classic experiment, Ivan Pavlov discovered he could get dogs to salivate at the ring of a bell by gradually substituting the sound for a spray of meat powder. Coca-Cola says that, just as Pavlov's dogs began to associate a new meaning with the bell, advertising is supposed to provide some new image or meaning for a product. Although the specifics of Coke's test are a secret, the company says it attempts to evaluate how well a commercial "conditions" a viewer to accept a positive image that can be transferred to the product. During the past three years, Coca-Cola says, ads that scored well in its tests almost always resulted in higher sales of soft drinks. "We nominate Pavlov as the father of modern advertising," says Joel S. Dubrow, communications research manager at Coke. "Pavlov took a neutral object and, by associating it with a meaningful object, made it a symbol of something else; he imbued it with imagery, he gave it added value." That, says Mr. Dubrow, "is what we try to do with modern advertising." ("Coca-Cola Turns to Pavlov," *Wall Street Journal*, January 19, 1984, p. 34)

While it isn't clear whether we buy things because of deep, hidden unconscious forces of the kind Freud and his followers discussed or because we've been subject to "conditioning" like one of Pavlov's dogs, or something else, one fact remains all-important—we've all bought something that an advertiser wanted us to buy as a result of some advertisement affecting our minds, our psyches, our emotions, and to some extent our rational thought processes.

Performance Based Advertising

Traditionally, advertising agencies received around 15 percent of the cost of an advertising campaign for their services. But in recent years, some corporations have switched to performance based advertising which rewards agencies according to whether certain goals have been reached. This may involve something like the percentage of the target audience reached or the number of responses to promotions or sales made that can be tied to the advertising campaign.

Pitch

This refers to attempts that advertising agencies make to potential clients to convince them to hire them to create advertisements for an advertising campaign. We can also say that actors and actresses in commercials are pitching whatever they are selling to us and doing everything they can to get us to decide to purchase what they are selling.

Political Advertising

We have had political advertising for many years, but in recent years, especially as a result of a Supreme Court decision, political advertising has become extremely important. *The New York Times* offers figures for the amount of money spent in the 2012 presidential campaign (elections.nytimes.com/2012/campaign-finance):

DEMOCRATS	REPUBLICANS
$ 1,072,600,000 raised	$ 992,500,000 raised
985,000,000 spent	992,000,000 spent

Approximately 2 billion dollars was raised by the two parties, and close to 2 billion dollars was spent by them. To these figures we can add the money spent on senate and house campaigns and other political campaigns. It is obvious that we spend enormous amounts of money for campaigns and that our politicians devote a great deal of time to obtaining money to run their campaigns.

Positioning

Positioning involves the process of creating an identity for a product in the minds of consumers, stressing its distinctive attributes, and showing how it compares favorably with competing products. Thus, for example, the Volvo is positioned in terms of being safe to drive and the iPhone in terms of its design and functionality.

Postmodernism

There are countless definitions of postmodernism, but most theorists of the subject suggest that it is connected to the rise of mass media and the new world of simulations and "hyperreality." Jean Baudrillard, a French sociologist, believed that media and simulated models have replaced manufacturing as the basic way of organizing societies.

As Steven Best and Douglas Kellner explain in *Postmodern Theory: Critical Interrogations* (1991, New York: Guilford, p. 119):

> For Baudrillard the models of the United States in Disneyland are more real than their instantiations in the social world, as the USA becomes more and more like Disneyland….The hyperreal for Baudrillard is a condition whereby models replace the real, as exemplified in such phenomena as the ideal home in women's or lifestyle magazines, ideal sex as portrayed in sex manuals.

Baudrillard, along with Roland Barthes and a number of other French theorists, has played a major role in the development of what we now call cultural theory. Postmodernism is important because in postmodern societies, there is a focus on consumption. Some postmodernist theorists argue that what we call postmodernism is really a name for an advanced form of capitalism. In principle, postmodernism became dominant in American culture around the sixties, replacing modernism.

We get a different perspective on Baudrillard's theories in a book edited by two archaeologists, Andrew Bevan and David Wengrow, *Cultures of Commodity Branding*. Their thesis is that branding is a very old phenomenon and not the result of modern capitalism. In their introduction, they describe Baudrillard's analysis of branding as follows (2010, Walnut Creek, CA: Left Coast Press, p. 14):

> Jean Baudrillard…saw modern branding practices as a form of cultural alchemy specific to capitalist modernity and unparalleled in earlier social formations. The brand sign, he argued, brings together in an ephemeral material form two conflicting

psychological tendencies: the drive for short term gratification and the long term need for transcendence—what we might call, for brevity's sake, the *Coca-Cola is Life* effect. The intended outcome is a short-lived transcendence of self that can only be sustained through further acts of purchase and consumption.

Baudrillard, like many other cultural theorists, may have been wrong about the origins of branding, but his discussion of the psychology of consumption helps us understand why it plays such an important role in our lives. It is a means for transcendence in people that is connected to dependencies tied to brands people covet and desire to own which lead them to become "hooked" on buying things and, in particular, brand name products. For Baudrillard consumption seems very much like drug addiction or any other kind of addiction. Bevan and Wengrow suggest that branding is similar in nature to ancient rituals tied to gift giving and sacrifices.

Baudrillard offers an insight into the way advertising works. We aren't influenced, he suggests, by any particular advertisement but by advertising's general impact on our culture and the regressive impulses advertising stimulates in us. He uses psychoanalytic theory, applied to groups, in his discussion of advertising in his book, *The System of Objects* (1968, London: Verso, p. 167):

> Neither its rhetoric nor even the information aspect of its discourse has a decisive effect on the buyer. What the individual does respond to, on the other hand, is advertising's underlying leitmotiv of protection and gratification, the intimation that its solicitations and attempts to persuade are the sign, indecipherable at the conscious level, that somewhere is an agency...which has taken it upon itself to inform him of his own desires, and to foresee and rationalize these desires to his own satisfaction. He thus no more "believes" in advertising than the child believes in Father Christmas, but this in no way impedes his capacity to embrace an internalized infantile situation, and to act accordingly. Herein lies the very real effectiveness of advertising,

founded on its obedience to a logic which, though not that of the conditioned reflex, is nonetheless very rigorous: a logic of belief and regression.

Baudrillard doesn't claim that advertising works by conditioning us but by temporarily regressing people to infantile states when their thought processes are not well developed and their desires can overwhelm their rationality.

Regression is a psychoanalytic concept that explains how in certain situations people regress or return to earlier stages in their development as a means of reinforcing their egos and helping them balance pressures from their desires (id elements in the psyche) and feelings of guilt (superego elements in the psyche). Freud's theories about sexuality help us understand why so many advertisements have beautiful women and handsome men in them—since they act as "turn ons" to repressed or sometimes hidden attitudes about sexuality and sexual desire for many people.

Price Sensitivity

People who are very concerned about the price of things they buy are "price sensitive." In supermarkets they tend to buy store brands, because they are less expensive than advertised brands. Price sensitive people also look for sales so they can save money on products or services they need or want. Some very wealthy people are not price sensitive. If they want something, they purchase it without being greatly concerned about its price. That explains why some very upscale stores don't have prices in their window displays. What they are saying is, in effect, "if you're concerned about the price, this shop is not for you." It isn't always the case that lower class (and poorer people) are more price sensitive than middle class or upper class people. Some wealthy people are price sensitive while some poor people "splurge" for expensive things they really want—if they can afford them, that is.

Product as Hero

This term is used for advertisements with a certain narrative design sometimes described as "product as hero" or a product/solution text. These advertisements involve posing a problem that viewers may be experiencing and then offering the product as the solution to the problem. In some cases, in product avoidance advertisements, the product is presented as a way to avoid a problem.

Product Placement

People in the advertising industry call the time taken up by commercials "clutter." There are so many commercials, one after another, that viewers often confuse one commercial with another. In *Buying In: What We Buy and Who We Are,* Rob Walker provides some insights into why product placement has become so important in advertising (2008, New York: Random House, pp. 128–129):

> In 2007, the media-buying firm Mindshare reported that the average amount of TV time taken up by either ads or network promotions had leveled off—at about fifteen minutes of every hour....Advertisers refer to it as "clutter."...The findings of another firm, TNS Media Intelligence, suggested that branding is increasingly escaping from the thirty-second confines of actual commercials and cluttering its way into shows themselves, in the form of paid product placements. In 2006, six minutes and twenty-two seconds of a typical prime-time hour were devoted to paid product placements—a leap of 89 percent over the prior year. On newly popular unscripted "reality" shows, the figure was closer to eleven minutes. In the third quarter of 2006, episodes of one CBS show, *Rock Star: Supernova,* included an astonishing 1,609 product or brand image shots.

The advantage of product placements is that people see the products during the show used by celebrities and actors and don't have discrete commercial breaks to zap using some device. Product placement is popular because so many people now time-shift their watching and can easily delete or fast forward through commercials.

Psychological Pricing

This technique is often used with expensive products to generate positive emotional responses in potential customers. This may be done by using glamorous models, movie stars, and other celebrities to sell a product and by offering arguments about the quality of the product to justify its high price. The price may be affected by the design and construction of the object, by the status of the manufacturer (Hermes, for example), and by other advertisements for it and competing products.

Q

Quick Cuts

"Quick cuts" is an editing technique in which many images follow one another in rapid succession. In his book, *Spots: The Popular Art of American Television Commercials,* Bruce Kurtz discusses the work of Dan Nichols, who made many McDonald's commercials and whose work is characterized by many quick cuts. Kurtz describes Nichols's "Quick Cuts" McDonald's advertisement as follows (1977, New York: Arts Communication, p. 94):

> Nichols' McDonald's spots possess the most accelerated time sense of any on television. "Quick Cuts" contains more cuts than can be counted: after repeated viewings the author had to

slow down the tape to count 65 different scenes in 60 seconds. A seven-second segment of this spot contains fourteen separate scenes, or two per second. Incredible as it may seem, it *is* possible for the viewer to perceive these different scenes even though they go by faster than can be counted....Because of the sense of urgency and of presentness which the spots communicate, the viewer actually experiences the exciting lifestyle Nichols depicts rather than passively observing events which occur to someone else....More than promoting a particular product, these spots advertise an appealing way of life associated with the restaurant, causing the viewer to turn to the product for gratification.

What Nichols does in his commercial is to create an appealing way of life that viewers of the commercials associate with McDonald's. The rapid pace of images, the quick cutting, generates a visceral excitement in viewers of these commercials that becomes attached to McDonald's. This discussion calls our attention to the importance of editing in commercials and texts of all kinds

R

Ratings and Shares

People who sell advertising make a distinction between shares and ratings. One of the best explanations of the difference between the two was made by Barry L. Sherman. When doing surveys dealing with what television programs people are watching, researchers distinguish between audience ratings and audience shares. Sherman explains the differences in *Telecommunications Management: Broadcasting/Cable and the New Technologies* (1995, New York: McGraw-Hill, p. 389):

> *Rating* refers to the percentage of people or households in an area tuned to a specific station, program, or network. For example, if, in a Nielsen sample of 1000 homes, 250 households were tuned to the ABC network, the rating for ABC during that time period would be (250 div 1000), or 25%. For ease of reporting, the percentage sign is dropped in the ratings book. *Share* refers to the number of people or households tuned to a particular station program or network correlated with sets in use. Continuing the above example, if only 750 of the sampled households were actually watching television in the time period covered, ABC's share would be (250 div 750) = 33%. Since there are always more sets in a market than there are sets in use, the share figure is always higher than the rating.

Radio stations, television stations, media networks, print publications, and now social media and internet sites make money by delivering audiences to advertisers. This means that the size and the nature of the audience reached (especially if it is age 18–49 males) help determine how much agencies pay to the media they use to place their advertisements and commercials.

Reception Theory

Reception theorists are literary scholars who have speculated about the role of "readers" in bringing texts, such as novels, to life. We can apply their theories to advertisements and commercials with relative ease. "Reception theory," also known as "reader response theory," deals with the role that readers of literary works—and by implication advertisements and commercials and all kinds of other texts—play in the scheme of things.

This theory was developed by a German literature professor, Wolfgang Iser, and his colleagues at the University of Constance in West Germany. It considers the "gaps" that exist in all literary works and the way literary texts stimulate readers to find or construct meanings in these texts that are not in the minds of the authors and not in the texts. This theory can be applied to the way people exposed to advertisements and commercials may be constructing their own meanings in the "gaps" in these texts—and the presumption is that all texts have "gaps" in them.

In Iser's essay, "The Reading Process: A Phenomenological Approach," (in David Lodge, Ed., 1988, *Modern Criticism and Theory: a Reader*, New York: Longman, p. 212):

> The phenomenological theory of art lays full stress on the idea that, in considering a literary work, one must take into account not only the actual text but also, and in equal measure, the actions involved in responding to that text. Thus Roman Ingarden confronts the structure of the literary text with the ways in which it can be *konkretisiert* (realized). The text as such offers different "schematized views" through which the subject matter of the work can come to light, but the actual bringing to light is an action of *konkretisation*. If this is so, then, the literary work has two poles, which we might call the artistic, and the aesthetic: the artistic refers to the text created by the author, and the aesthetic to the realization accomplished by the reader. From this polarity it follows that the literary work cannot be completely

identical with the text, or with the realization of the text, but in fact must lie halfway between the two. The work is more than the text, for the text only takes on life when it is realized, and furthermore the realization is by no means independent of the individual disposition of the reader—though this in turn is acted upon by the different patterns of the text. This convergence of text and reader brings the literary work into existence, and this convergence can never be precisely pinpointed, but must always remain virtual, as it is not to be identified either with the reality of the text or with the individual disposition of the reader.

Iser makes an important point in this lengthy and difficult passage. He suggests that texts, and texts we are interested in here are advertisements and commercials, and their readers/viewers are two opposites, and in between is the "work," which is the understanding the reader has of the text.

The diagram below shows this relationship:

Text	WORK	Reader
Print Ad/Commercial	WORK	Reader/Viewer

The Print Ad/Commercial only comes into existence, we can say, when perceived by a Reader/Viewer, and what we get from this process is what Iser calls the work. There is not an automatic understanding of texts by their readers. Readers bring their dispositions, personalities, and cultural understandings to texts in creating WORKS.

The problem artists and copywriters in advertising agencies face involves creating texts that will lead to the desired kind of WORKS or understanding in the minds of readers and viewers exposed to their advertisements and commercials. What we learn from Iser is that authors only create part of a work; readers are needed to bring the work into existence and make sense of it. And this is because all texts have "gaps" in them which readers/viewers fill with their own ideas and beliefs.

Although reception theory may be seen as an extremely involved and abstruse theory, it does have enormous relevance for "creatives" in advertising agencies because it explains why people decode advertising "incorrectly" or in ways not perceived or expected by the artists and writers who create advertisements and commercials. What we learn from Iser is that there is no one correct, objective interpretation of any text; different people read a given text different ways. They may get certain ideas in common from the text, but they also read different things in the text, in part because all texts are constructed of conscious and unconscious intertextual citations from previous texts and because they have so many "gaps" in them which readers fill in. These texts also connect to cultural codes, either conscious or unconscious, that affect the way people react to texts.

Since many advertisements have images in them, and commercials generally have people in them and a narrative structure, getting audiences to interpret these texts the way writers and artists want them to becomes even more difficult. What complicates things even further is that texts of all kinds are very rich and have many different levels of meaning. Yuri Lotman, a semiotician from Tartu, Estonia, explains in his book, *The Structure of the Artistic Text* (1977, Ann Arbor: Michigan Slavic Contributions, p. 17), "The tendency to interpret *everything* in an artistic text as meaningful is so great that we might rightfully consider nothing accidental in a work of art." He adds (p. 23):

> Since it can concentrate a tremendous amount of information into the "area" of a very small text (c.f. the length of a short story by Chekov and a psychology textbook), an artistic text manifests yet another feature: it transmits different information to different readers in proportion to each one's comprehension: it provides the reader with a language in which each successive portion of information may be assimilated with repeated reading. It behaves as a kind of living organism which has a feedback channel to the reader and thereby instructs him.

We learn two important things from Lotman: one, everything in a text is meaningful and nothing is accidental, and two, the more you know, the more you can find in a text. Because artistic texts are so rich, we can reread them or see them again and each time we get more out of them and find different things in them. We can say the same thing about advertisements and commercials.

Rhetoric

According to Aristotle, rhetoric is the art of convincing others. As he explained in his *Rhetoric* (quoted in Richard McKeon, 1941, *The Basic Works of Aristotle,* New York: Random House, p. 1329):

> Rhetoric may be defined as the faculty of observing in any given case the available means of persuasion. This is not a function of any other art. Every other art can instruct or persuade about its own particular subject-matter; for instance, medicine about what is healthy and unhealthy, geometry about the properties of magnitudes, arithmetic about numbers, and the same is true of the other arts and sciences. But rhetoric we look upon as the power of observing the means of persuasion on almost any subject presented to us; and that is why we say that, in its technical character, it is not concerned with any special or definite class of subjects.

Advertising is based on linguistic and visual persuasion, so advertising copywriters are, from Aristotle's perspective, rhetoricians. He suggests three modes of persuasion in rhetoric, what he called Ethos, Pathos and Logos:

Means of Persuasion	Persuasion Tied To
Ethos	Speaker has credibility
Pathos	Speaker stirs emotions in listeners
Logos	Speaker makes logical arguments

In many television commercials we now find physicians suggesting we ask our physicians about (that is, have them prescribe) certain medicines. These commercials use all three of Aristotle's modes of persuasion: *Ethos*: Doctors talking about medicines have credibility; *Pathos*: Doctors stir emotions in viewers about the seriousness of the disease being discussed; and *Logos*: Doctors suggest that the medicine they are discussing will possibly help many people (and also additional *Pathos* since these medicines all have many serious negative side effects).

Americans have been interested in and concerned about the role advertising plays in our society and culture, and there have been many books written over the years warning Americans about the persuasive power of advertising. One of the most celebrated was Vance Packard's *The Hidden Persuader*, published in 1957. In his book Packard warned his readers about the power of advertising (New York: David McKay, p. 3):

> This book is an attempt to explore a strange and rather exotic new area of American life. It is about the way many of us are being influenced and manipulated—far more than we realize—in the patterns of our everyday lives. Large-scale efforts are being made, often with impressive success, to channel our unthinking habits, our purchasing decisions, and our thought processes by the use of insights gleaned from psychiatry and the social sciences. Typically these efforts take place beneath our level of awareness; so that the appeals which move us are often, in a sense, hidden.
>
> Some of this manipulating being attempted is simply amusing. Some of it is disquieting, particularly when viewed as a portent of what may be ahead on a more intensive and effective scale for us all. Co-operative scientists have come along providentially to furnish some awesome tools.

For Packard, the use of psychoanalytic and other methods has enabled advertisers to be more effective in selling us "products, ideas, attitudes, candidates, goals or states of mind" (p. 3). Since Packard wrote his book, in 1957, the advertising industry has developed many new ways of understanding our thought processes and new methods of attempting to shape our behavior.

S

Semiotics

Semiotics is defined as the science of signs, which means it focuses upon the role of signs in society and, in particular, how people find meaning in various aspects of life. If advertisers are to communicate with their target audiences effectively, they must know how these target audiences think and the way they interpret signs and symbols. One problem is that we know that people don't always interpret advertisements the way the people who create the ads expect them to. A number of years ago I met the president of an advertising agency in Britain who told me that people in his agency were very interested in semiotics, just as many semioticians are very interested in advertising.

Ferdinand de Saussure and C. S. Peirce are the founding fathers of the science of semiotics, which deals with signs (the term "sēmeîon" means sign) and how people find meaning in them. A sign is anything that can be used to stand for something else. Thus, if we look at a print advertisement with a male and female model and textual material in it, everything in that advertisement can be considered a sign: the bodies of the man and the woman, the clothes they are wearing, their facial expressions, the color of their hair, the style of their hair, their body language, the content of the textual material, the typography used in the textual material, the spatiality of the advertisement, ad infinitum.

In Saussure's book, *Course in General Linguistics,* he called his science semiology—literally, words about signs. In one of the foundational descriptions of the science of signs, he writes (1915/1966, New York: McGraw-Hill, p. 16):

> Language is a system of signs that express ideas, and is therefore comparable to a system of writing, the alphabet of deaf-mutes, symbolic rites, polite formulas, military signals, etc. But it is the most important of all these systems.
>
> *A science that studies the life of signs within society* is conceivable; it would be a part of social psychology and consequently of general psychology; I shall call it *semiology* (from Greek *sēmeîon* "sign"). Semiology would show what constitutes signs, what laws govern them. Since the science does not yet exist, no one can say what it would be; but it has a right to existence, a place staked out in advance.

This statement opens the study of all kinds of communication to us, for not only can we study symbolic rites and military signals, we can also study soap operas, situation comedies, and advertisements and commercials—and almost anything else—as "sign systems."

He also explained what signs were: "The linguistic sign unites not a thing and a name, but a concept and a sound-image....I call the combination of a concept and a sound-image a *sign,* but in current usage the term generally designates only a sound-image" (pp. 66–67). He divided signs into two components, a *signifier* (or "sound-image") and a *signified* (or "concept"), and pointed out that the relationship between signifier and signified is arbitrary; these points were of crucial importance for the development of semiotics. He offered another idea of consequence—namely that concepts have no meaning in themselves. The meaning of concepts depends on the way they are different from their opposites.

As he explained (p. 118):

Concepts are purely differential and defined not by their positive content but negatively by their relations with the other terms of the system. Their most precise characteristic is in being what the others are not....Signs function, then, not through their intrinsic value but through their relative position.

Later, he added, "Everything that has been said to this point boils down to this: in languages there are only differences" (p. 120). The most important difference, it turns out, is the bipolar opposition: hot and cold, rich and poor, beautiful and ugly, hero and villain. As Saussure wrote, "The entire mechanism of language... is based on oppositions" (p. 121). It is the very nature of language that makes us see things in terms of oppositions, and thus, concepts, for Saussure, mean something by not being their opposite. When we see an advertisement or a commercial, or any text, our minds function, automatically and involuntarily, to sort out the various oppositions: hero or villain, beautiful or ugly, something to buy or something to ignore.

The second founding father of semiotics, and the thinker who gave the science its name, semiotics, was Charles Peirce, who made an important distinction between three different kinds of signs: icons, indexes, and symbols. *Icons* signify by resemblance; *indexes* signify by cause and effect; and *symbols* signify on the basis of convention. As Peirce wrote:

Every sign is determined by its objects, either first by partaking in the characters of the object, when I call a sign an *Icon;* secondly, by being really and in its individual existence connected with the individual object, when I call the sign an *Index;* thirdly, by more or less approximate certainty that it will be interpreted as denoting the object, in consequence of a habit (which term I use as including a natural disposition), when I call the sign a *Symbol.* (Quoted in J. J. Zeman, "Pierce's Theory of Signs," in T. A.

Sebeok, Ed., *A Perfusion of Signs*, 1977, Bloomington: Indiana University Press, p. 36)

The following chart offers examples of each kind of sign in Peirce's theory:

	Icons	Indexes	Symbols
Signify by:	Resemblance	Cause and effect	Convention
Example:	Photograph	Fire and smoke	Cross, Flags
Process:	Can see	Can figure out	Must learn

We can see that there are differences between Saussure's science of signs and Peirce's, although both deal with signs and both theories have been very influential. Peirce also said a sign "is something which stands to somebody for something in some respect or capacity," which means that meaning is always created by individuals (quoted in Zeman, p. 27). He also argued that the universe is "perfused with signs, if it is not composed exclusively of signs" (epigraph in Sebeok, p. vi). This suggests that since everything in the universe is a sign, semiotics is the "master" science!

Semiotics has been of considerable use to scholars dealing with advertising, since it helps us figure out how people find meaning in advertisements and commercials, and it is useful to people in the advertising industry who are interested in the same topic. There are a number of semiotic analyses of advertising, such as Marshall McLuhan's *The Mechanical Bride* (though he doesn't mention semiotics or use semiotic concepts, his analysis is semiotic in nature) and Judith Williamson's *Decoding Advertisements: Ideology and Meaning in Advertising*. When you see the term "meaning" being used in a book's title, there usually is a connection with semiotics.

Semiotics argues that we are always sending messages to others about ourselves, and others are sending messages about themselves to us. Semiotics has the goal of understanding the full significance of these messages and messages we get from advertisements and commercials, and how all these messages are interpreted or "decoded" by other people. One problem with signs is that they can be used to lie, which means that blonde you see may be a brunette and that man you see may be a woman and that woman you see may be a man. It is because we know that signs lie that we must become suspicious of all signs and of the advertisements and commercials that employ them so artfully.

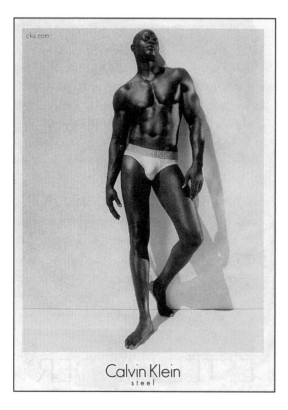

This Calvin Klein advertisement for underwear exploits the male body the way many advertisements exploit the female body: to sell products—in this case, underwear. It is only in recent years that the male body has been presented in advertisements as an object of sexual desire or lust.

Sexploitation

Until recently, sexploitation referred to advertisements that exploit the female body and female sexual allure to sell products and services. In recent years, the male body has been used for the same purposes. This is a relatively new phenomenon—exposing the male body to the desire and lust of others, male and female, I would presume—and the Calvin Klein advertisements provide an excellent example of this. There is no advertising copy other than the brand name and the product's name, which means the image must do all the selling.

Shopping

Why people buy what they buy and how shopping relates to the way people purchase products and services are an enigma that fascinates everyone in the advertising business. There are countless books on the subject. Among the most interesting recent ones are:

Paco Underhill. *Why We Buy: The Science of Shopping*

Rob Walker. *Buying In: What We Buy and Who We Are*

Lee Eisenberg, *Shoptimism: Why the American Consumer Will Keep on Buying No Matter What*

Gerald Zaltman. *How Customers Think: Essential Insights into the Mind of the Market*

Herb Sorensen. *Inside The Mind of the Shopper: The Science of Retailing*

These books, and many others, deal with how people shop and why they purchase what they buy. As I explained in an article I wrote about shopping, "Shop un á Son Gout" (a pun on the French "chaçun a son gout" or "to each his own taste") that appeared in *Society* magazine (8[2], March/April 2011, pp. 112–116):

There is probably no animal, with the exception of the laboratory rat, that is studied with such feverish attention as the human

In this advertisement for Trump International, we have an image of the dilemma of choice that many shoppers feel: it is very difficult to decide which shoes to purchase when we have so many opportunities. Trump focuses on this and reminds us that Trump is where we can find the kinds of shoes a fashionable woman would want to purchase.

shopper—*homo consumens.* Paco Underhill relates in his book how he has shot 50,000 videos a year of people shopping, recorded numberless interviews with shoppers, and collected countless "track sheets" of his employees surreptitiously following people and noting their every move as they wandered through various kinds of stores.

Shopping, sometimes known as "retail therapy," is an all-consuming (in every sense of the term) passion with many people. There are two main schools of thought that explain our purchasing decisions. One school argues that they are based on our personalities and our psyches—our desire to be admired and loved, our wish to improve our lives, our hope to be envied, among other motivations. Ernest

Dichter and many other psychologists and psychoanalysts are in this first school. The other school argues that our purchasing decisions are tied to our lifestyles and the groups we belong to, and that what we buy is tied to the unconscious imperatives in each lifestyle. Mary Douglas, the British anthropologist, is a thinker from the second school. Shopping, she reminds us, is not a matter of personal choice but of obeying the generally unrecognized dictates of one's lifestyle.

A survey of 12,500 Americans made by the U.S. Bureau of Labor Statistics shows that the amount of time we spend shopping dropped to 43.2 minutes a day in 2011 from 45 minutes a day in 2010. But because of internet sites like Amazon.com, it is possible to view many different products and purchase what is desired with little more than the click of a mouse. This means we can shop more quickly. As a result of trends like this, many so-called "bricks and mortar" establishments—that is, actual stores—have developed internet sites and are now "bricks and clicks" establishments.

Sign Wars

This refers to advertising wars between category leading products such as Coca-Cola and Pepsi-Cola and different brands of sneakers—and now smart phones such as the iPhone and the Samsung Galaxy SIII. These campaign battles are advertising's moral equivalent of war. There is a book, *Sign Wars: Cluttered Landscape of Advertising,* by Robert Goldman and Stephen Papson that deals with the various battles between competing products and with problems advertising agencies face in their desperate attempt to attract the attention of desired target audiences. The authors tie sign wars to semiotics in the first chapter of the book (1996, New York: Guilford, p. 25):

> Advertisers often work in ways mindful of how the pioneer of semiotics, Saussure, approached his task, slicing everything into paired categories. Advertisers frequently define their positioning category by juxtaposing it against a negative signifier. One way to

define sign value is in terms of what it is *not*....Sign wars represent a mature stage of brand completion. With each successive round of sign competition, semiotics has become increasingly annexed as a tool and foregrounded as substance.

According to the authors, advertising agencies are continually struggling with one another for the public's eye and ear and with the problem of clutter, which causes audiences to forget the messages from advertisers. The saturation of messages means that audiences of advertisements and commercials often cannot differentiate between one commercial and the next and often become bored with them. Advertisers then become increasingly desperate to find ways to get their messages across, and engage in activities that are ultimately self-defeating. As the authors point out in the last page of their book (p. 274):

> In the "simulacrum" of television advertising, the sign of difference replaces difference. In the whirl of sign wars, advertising generates a glut of signs that makes it difficult to differentiate those signs. Fueling this motor of cultural appropriation requires the constant sacrifice of "unpolluted meaning systems." This pollution process and the constant rerouting of meanings of authenticity, identity and resistance has taken a deep toll on our culture: it has cost us our faith.

Goldman and Papson are quite pessimistic about the impact of advertising on our culture and society; they may be too pessimistic, for if theorists like de Certeau are correct, people have ways of combating advertising, and if Umberto Eco is correct, most people decode the advertising to which they are exposed aberrantly.

Slogans

Slogans are catchy phrases meant to convey some quality of a product being advertised that consumers will remember. L'Oreal's slogan "Because You're Worth It" generates certain feelings in women and suggests that even if L'Oreal products might be expensive, using them is a good idea because the women using their products are "worth" it, and so are the products. Gel Color by Opi tells readers "Color at the Speed of Life," a play on the speed of light. Movado announces it is "Modern Ahead of Its Time." Tiffany & Co. explains it is "Legendary for 175 Years." The Sunglass Hut tells us "You Don't Need Words To Make a Statement," which offers an insight into how people use sunglasses—to shield their eyes but also to convey messages about their sense of style. In 2013 during the Emmys we find Pepsi telling us "Live for Now," Diet Pepsi imploring us to "Love Every Sip," Chevrolet asking us to "Find New Roads," and Taco Bell reminding us to "Live Mas" (more). Some slogans are short lived, while others can last for years.

Slogans are phrases meant to be memorable that advertisers use to create awareness of their products and to generate certain emotional feelings towards the products. Often these slogans characterize an entire campaign for a product. McDonald's "You, You're the One" and "I'm Lovin It" would be examples of slogans. Slogans are meant to leave viewers of commercials with certain ideas and feelings about the product being advertised—ideas and feelings that they will remember and that will resonate with them, especially material buried in the unconscious realms of their psyches.

Social Media

Internet sites such as Facebook, Twitter, Google+, and countless others are the most important development in recent years for advertising agencies. As a former student of mine who worked in one of the best agencies in San Francisco told me, "Everyone at the agency is focused on social media now." The various internet sites make money by selling advertising of one kind or another to companies that advertise on them, and because they are such a gigantic source of "eyeballs," of people tuned into them, and because people spend so much time on these social media, they are now an increasingly important medium for advertising. They also play an important role in many people's everyday lives. Sites such as Twitter have been used by revolutionaries in many countries to organize people and plan their rallies.

Socio-Economic Class

For many years, many Americans thought that class was irrelevant, since the American Dream said that everyone can get ahead if they are willing to work hard enough. We had, it was thought, an essentially all middle-class country, except for small numbers of wealthy people and "pockets" of poverty. In recent years, we have become aware of the importance of class and there have been many articles dealing with the fact that the top 1 percent of the American population owns something like 40 percent of the wealth in this country.

In 1953, W. Lloyd Warner, a distinguished sociologist, suggested that there are six classes in American society. His estimates of the distribution of membership in these classes in the population of the United States follow:

Upper-upper	1.4%	
Lower-upper	1.6%	
Upper-middle	10%	
Lower-middle	28%	common man and woman level
Upper-lower	33%	common man and woman level
Lower-lower	25%	

The figures above are more than fifty years old, but they give us a picture of the class makeup of American society that is still fairly accurate. There are a number of factors that determine socio-economic class, such as education, income, and occupation. What is important for us to recognize is that different social classes have different lifestyles, different ways of raising children, different values, and are affected by advertising in different ways.

Economists estimate now that the wealthiest 1 percent of American families own more than 40 percent of all the corporate stock in the country, and the top 10 percent control almost 70 percent of the total wealth, including real estate corporate stocks and business assets. There are approximately 80 million families in the United States, but 400,000 households control more than a quarter of the wealth. Thus, although many Americans tend to think of the United States as essentially middle-class, it is instead a highly stratified, class-based society. Although a substantial middle class exists, the members of the economic elite in the United States definitely have enormous political power. Advertising agencies face the problem of figuring out how to appeal to the different classes. In some cases, there isn't a problem, because very upscale products generally are purchased by members of the upper classes, who can easily decode the advertisements directed to them. In products and services directed to a number of different classes, finding ways to appeal to them is more of a problem. Umberto Eco, a prominent semiotician, suggests that most people do not understand (decode) messages correctly. He calls this "aberrant decoding" and says it is the norm for most people. For many years, Americans believed we were essentially a classless society, with a large middle class and a smaller elite class and some so-called pockets of poverty. In recent years, we've become aware of the amount of inequality in the United States and of the economic and political power of the top 1 percent in society. That is, we've become much more aware of the existence of different classes in the United States and the role these classes play in our political and social order.

Storyboards

Storyboards are large boards on which the key images in a television commercial are drawn—to give people in advertising agencies and corporations that have hired an agency an idea of what a particular commercial will look like. Here I show the storyboard for a Levi's commercial, "The Stranger," which had an interesting religious overtone to it. When you watch the actual commercial, you realize how primitive storyboards are and how they only give you a vague idea of what the commercial will actually be like.

Subliminal Advertising

This theory argues that advertisers often insert subliminally apprehended messages, through images and words in their texts

Soft Whiskey à la mode.

The hardest thing about it is the rocks.

According to Wilson Bryan Key, the ice cubes in advertisements contain subliminal messages, full of sexual symbols that resonate in our unconscious. That would explain why this advertisement for Calvert shows the ice cubes so prominently.

that have the power to evade our conscious and rational thought processes to achieve their ends. Wilson Bryan Key has written a book, *Subliminal Seduction: Ad Media's Manipulation of a Not So Innocent America.* On the cover, which shows a glass of liquor and some ice cubes, we read: *Are You Being Sexually Aroused By This Picture? Here are the ways ad men arouse your desires—to sell their products.*

In the beginning of the book, which has an introduction by Marshall McLuhan, Key writes (1973, New York: Signet, p. 1):

Every person reading this book has been victimized and manipulated by the use of subliminal stimuli directed into his unconscious mind by the mass merchandizers of the media. The techniques are in widespread use by media, advertising, industrial and commercial corporations, and by the Federal

Government itself. The secret has been well kept. The average citizen, as well as most social and behavioral scientists, simply do not know what is going on.

From Key's perspective, subliminal "seduction" is not confined to an occasional advertisement or commercial, but is ubiquitous. He continues (p. 3):

> This book acknowledges the role of conscious perception, but will concentrate upon *unconscious* perception—subliminal experiences which manipulate, manage or control human behavior, but of which humans are consciously unaware....This book is concerned only with content planted within media which readers or audiences are *not supposed to see or read,* at least at the conscious level.

Key's discussion reminds us of Freud's analysis of the human psyche which I represented, in my discussion of his theories, by an iceberg. What Key argues is that much material we are exposed to, that is subliminal in nature, goes directly into our unconscious and bypasses our awareness. This material generally involves images and words. Subliminal messages are functional only as long as we are unaware of them.

Key then offers an analysis of a Gilbey's Gin print advertisement featuring ice cubes in which he finds all kinds of hidden messages— and some not so hidden. He examines the ice cubes and finds in them the letters S, E and X, forming the word sex. Key suggests that we find all kinds of hidden sexual turn-ons in the images found in ice cubes in liquor advertisements: skeletons, snakes, letters, and other similar phenomena connected with our obsession with love and death.

In his chapter on symbolization, he offers a list of male and female symbols that reminds us of Freud's analysis of the symbols in dreams (p. 58):

> In the mass media of communication, the preoccupation with love and death symbolism is apparent in every newspaper,

magazine, and television program. Genital is universally used in the media, though rarely recognized by the audience as such. Commonly used phallic symbolism includes neckties, arrows, flagpoles, automobiles, rockets, pencils, cigars and cigarettes, candles, broomsticks, snakes, trees, canons, pens—the list is endless. Vaginal symbols are developed from virtually any round or elliptical shape—lips, eyes, belt buckles, the oval feminine face surrounded by hair, apples, pears, oranges, cherries, balls, eggs—again the list is extensive.

Key's point is that sexually suggestive symbolization pervades the media and that these symbols are part of the campaign of subliminal seduction waged against people by advertisers. *Subliminal Seduction* is, as you might imagine, a very controversial book. Most people in the advertising industry would say they do not practice subliminal advertising, by which they mean inserting extremely short and generally not noticeable images or words and phrases into commercials. From time to time advertisers do play tricks like this, but it is not commonly done. From Key's perspective, all advertising is subliminal in nature in that it stems from forces hidden in our unconscious of which we are unaware. At the end of his book Key argues that "media has the proven, completely established ability to program human behavior much in the same way as hypnosis" (p. 187). That statement strikes me as somewhat overdrawn, but Key does raise our awareness of the complex ways in which words and images affect our psyches, and he offers some interesting analyses of a number of advertisements.

Key finds all kinds of sexual imagery in ice cubes and the word "sex" in one particular advertisement. Can you find the word "sex" in this advertisement shown at the beginning of this definition? If you can, do you think it is an accident or the design of a crafty art director seeking to manipulate people? What sexual symbols do you find in this advertisement?

Symbols

One of the most interesting analyses of symbols can be found in a history classic, Johan Huizinga's *The Waning of the Middle Ages*. Although Huizinga was studying life in the Middle Ages, his insights into the nature and power of symbolism are worth considering. He writes (1954, Garden City, NY: Anchor, pp. 201–202):

> The Middle Ages never forgot that all things would be absurd, if their meaning were exhausted in their function and their place in the phenomenal world, if by their essence they did not reach into a world beyond this. This idea of a deeper significance in ordinary things is familiar to us as well, independently of religious convictions: as an indefinite feeling which may be called up at any moment, by the sound of raindrops on the leaves or by the lamplight on the table....."When we see all things in God, and refer all things to Him, we read in common matters superior expressions of meaning." [William James: *Varieties of Religious Experience*, p. 475] Here, then is the psychological foundation from which symbolism arises. In God nothing is empty of sense....So the conviction of a transcendental meaning in all things seeks to formulate itself. About the figure of the Divinity a majestic system of correlated figures crystallizes, which all have reference to Him, because all things derive their meaning from Him. The world unfolds itself like a vast whole of symbols, like a cathedral of ideas. It is the most richly rhythmical conception of the world, a polyphonous expression of eternal harmony.

We no longer see the world the way people did in the Middle Ages, when everything had a symbolic and religious meaning, but symbols still play an important role in our thinking and behavior. And that is because symbols have an impact upon our emotions and are connected to the very deepest and often hidden elements in our psyches. Some symbols are personal, but many are collective—such as those we learn from religious experience. From Charles Peirce (see definition of "semiotics") we learned that the meaning of a symbol must be learned; the meanings of symbols are conventional; we do not naturally know the meaning of symbols. Symbols are often connected to religious experiences and historical events and come to have a profound significance for us as we grow up.

The term "symbol" comes from the Greek *symbolon* which means token or sign. It also stands for something in the unconscious mind that has been repressed. It is that aspect of symbols that is important to us in our analysis of advertisements—their use of symbols to react with material already stored in our unconscious and trigger desires. Our dreams, Freud suggests are composed of symbols that we later stitch together into a dream narrative. Dream symbols are personal. One cannot compose a list of dream symbols that can be used to interpret all dreams for everyone—or even all advertisements—although, as Freud pointed out, some symbols, generally connected to our sexual nature, have a psychoanalytic significance to all of us.

It's worth considering what Clifford Geertz writes about symbols in *The Interpretation of Cultures* (1977, New York: Basic Books, p. 45):

Thinking consists not of "happenings in the head" (though happenings there and elsewhere are necessary for it to occur) but of a traffic in what have been called, by G. H. Mead and others—significant symbols—words for the most part but also gestures, drawings, musical sounds, mechanical devices like clocks, or natural objects like jewels—anything, in fact, that is disengaged from its mere actuality and used to impose meaning upon experience. From the point of view of any particular individual, such symbols are largely given. He finds them already current in the community in which is he is born, and they remain, with some additions, subtractions, and partial alterations he may or may not have had a hand in, in circulation when he dies. While he lives he uses them, or some of them, sometimes deliberately and with care, most often spontaneously and with ease, but always with the same end in view: to put a construction upon the events through which he lives, to orient himself within "the ongoing course of experiencing things," to adopt a vivid phrase of John Dewey's.

So symbols play an important role in communication of all kinds, and for our purposes, in advertising, which, for its own purposes, "imposes meaning on experience." Much of what we call thinking involves using, considering, manipulating, and analyzing symbols.

Synecdoche

"Synecdoche" is a weaker form of metonymy (defined earlier) in which a part stands for the whole or the whole stands for a part. Thus, the Pentagon stands for the entire American military, and Uncle Sam stands for the United States. We must recognize that metaphor and metonymy, and their weaker forms simile and synecdoche, are all pervasive in advertising and often occur in the same advertisement or commercial.

T

Target Audiences

These are audiences that are targeted by marketers and advertising agencies as being most appropriate for being exposed to advertising for certain products and services. Thus, elderly people are "target audiences" for pharmaceutical companies selling medicines for diseases of old age, and teenagers are "target audiences" for companies selling soft drinks, fast foods, electronic devices, and so on.

U

USP or Unique Selling Proposition

A "unique selling proposition" can be understood to be the one aspect of your product or service that is different from and better than products or services from your competitors. In Martin Mayer's *Madison Avenue U.S.A.* we find a discussion of this matter. He writes about Rosser Reeves, who helped develop the USP concept, as follows (1959, New York: Harper and Row, p. 49):

> "We can't sell a product," Reeves says, "unless it's a good product, and even then we can't sell it unless we can find the Unique Selling Proposition. There are three rules for a USP. First, you need a definite proposition: buy this product and you'll get this specific benefit. Pick up any textbook on advertising and that's what's on page one—but everybody ignores it. Then, second, it must be a unique proposition, one which the opposition *cannot* or *does not offer*. Third, the proposition must sell."

Reeves then discusses how Colgate advertised that its dental crème came out as a ribbon and was flat on one's toothbrush. It was a USP, but it didn't sell. It was when Colgate came up with its "cleans your breath while it cleans your teeth" slogan that it found a USP that sold well and gave it a large share of the market. Mayer writes, "USP's grow out of analyses of the product and what it can perform for its users: the result of the analysis of a single specific claim which will be repeated over and over again" (p. 49).

One difficulty in using the USP is that many products are similar to one another and it is difficult to find something really different. In cases like that, advertising agencies create or invent unique selling points, what can be described as "uncheckable claims," in an effort to differentiate the products they are selling from other products. Miller Lite's "Less filling, tastes great" slogan would be a good example of an uncheckable claim, and there are countless other advertising slogans that are similar in nature to the Miller slogan.

V

VALS Typology (See Claritas)

Arnold Mitchell, director of the Stanford Research Institute's (SRI) Values and Lifestyle Program, published a book in 1983 titled *The Nine American Lifestyles: Who We Are & Where We Are Going*. In his preface, he makes some interesting points (1983, New York: Macmillan, p. vii):

> People's values and lifestyles say a good deal about where we are going, and they help explain such practical, diverse questions as: why we support some issues and oppose others; why some people are strong leaders and others weak; why some people are economically brilliant and others gifted artistically—and a few are both; why we trust some people and are suspicious of others; why some products attract us and others don't; why revolutions occur.
>
> By the term "values" we mean the entire constellation of a person's attitudes, beliefs, opinions, hopes, fears, prejudices, needs, desires, and aspirations that, taken together, govern how one behaves....We now have powerful evidence that the classification of an individual on the basis of a few dozen attitudes and demographics tells us a good deal about what to expect of that person in hundreds of other domains. Further, the approach often enables us to identify the decisive quality-of-life factor or factors in a person's life.

Based on an extensive survey Mitchell and his colleagues conducted in 1984, SRI developed the VALS typology, which argues that there are eight groups of consumers who share similar values that shape their behavior.

The advertising industry was extremely interested in the VALS typology because advertising agencies thought it would help them target certain groups of interest to them and help them create more effective print advertisements and commercials. The argument SRI makes is that there is not one general American public but many different groupings, each of which is susceptible to different kinds of appeals by advertising agencies. This typology focuses on people's lifestyles rather than on demographic statistics. It is based on theories of psychological development and argues that there are eight different and distinctive kinds of American consumers. This is important, SRI suggests, because advertisers can target their appeals to the specific values of each kind of consumer. The data in VALS came from a survey it gave to 1,600 people.

The VALS typology was of interest to advertising agencies in the 1980s but now has more or less fallen out of favor. A typology by Claritas, discussed earlier, has gone beyond the VALS typology with a typology of sixty-six kinds of American consumers. In all these marketing typologies, the underlying notion is that they will help advertisers know their target audiences better and be able to focus the advertising they create to appeal to these groups.

Value Chain

This concept, used often in strategic planning, was developed by a Harvard Business School professor, Michael Porter, in his 1970 book, *Competitive Advantage: Creating and Sustaining Superior Performance* (New York: Free Press). A "value chain" refers to the series of activities a company carries out to provide a valuable product or service to its customers.

Viral Marketing

Let me quote from webmarketingtoday.com/articles/viral-principles/, which has an excellent description of viral marketing:

> What does a virus have to do with marketing? Viral marketing describes any strategy that encourages individuals to pass on a marketing message to others, creating the potential for exponential growth in the message's exposure and influence. Like viruses, such strategies take advantage of rapid multiplication to explode the message to thousands, to millions.
>
> Off the Internet, viral marketing has been referred to as "word-of-mouth," "creating a buzz," "leveraging the media," "network marketing." But on the Internet, for better or worse, it's called "viral marketing." While others smarter than I have attempted to rename it, to somehow domesticate and tame it, I won't try. The term "viral marketing" has stuck.

The theory behind viral marketing is that if you can create a video or whatever that strikes people's attention and which they forward to their friends, eventually you'll reach a large audience. Typically viral marketing relies upon social media—for example, a video or commercials that strike a chord with people and which they forward to their friends. The problem with viral marketing is that it is extremely difficult to create texts that "go viral."

Visual Persuasion

Advertising can be considered, among other things, a form of visual persuasion. Advertisements are created to sell people products and services. We know that words and metaphors are important, but so are images. There is an important book on advertising by Paul Messaris, *Visual Persuasion: The Role of Images in Advertising,* that deals with images and the role they play. Messaris suggests that images can play three major roles in advertising texts (1997, Thousand Oaks, CA: Sage, p. vii):

They can elicit emotions by simulating the appearance of a real person or object: they can serve as photographic proof that something really did happen; and they can establish an implicit link between the thing that is being sold and some other images. I will argue below that these three functions of advertising images stem from underlying fundamental characteristics of visual communication—characteristics that define the essential nature of images and distinguish them from language and from other modes of human communication. In turn, these three functions of advertising images give rise to a wide variety of specific advertising practices, ranging from celebrity endorsements to hidden-camera interviews to shots of politicians standing before flags.

These three roles can lead to an astonishing variety of different kinds of advertisements and commercials that Messaris deals with in his book. His book is divided into three parts: images as simulated reality, images as evidence, and images as implied selling propositions. Messaris alerts us to the incredible power images have over us and that, together with clever language, compelling metaphors, and other figures of speech, advertisements and commercials must be seen as formidable means of shaping consumer emotions and behavior.

The semiotician Yuri Lotman explained that everything in a text is important. As he wrote in his *The Structure of the Artistic Text*: "The tendency to interpret everything in an artistic text as meaningful is so great that we might rightfully consider nothing accidental in a work of art" (1977, Ann Arbor: Michigan Slavic Contributions, p. 17). If this is the case, advertisements and commercials must be seen as extremely complicated texts in which nothing is accidental and everything is important. Lotman may have overstated his case, but his point is worth considering: every image we find in an advertisement or television commercial and every word and everything else in these texts is there for a reason. This means that we must look upon these texts as complicated problems to analyze and explain. And we make our analyses by using all the techniques and methodologies discussed in this book.

About the Author

Arthur Asa Berger is Professor Emeritus of Broadcast and Electronic Communication Arts at San Francisco State University. He has published 70 books and more than 100 articles. He can be reached at: arthurasaberger@gmail.com.

green press
INITIATIVE

Left Coast Press, Inc. is committed to preserving ancient forests and natural resources. We elected to print this title on 30% post consumer recycled paper, processed chlorine free. As a result, for this printing, we have saved:

1 Trees (40' tall and 6-8" diameter)
1 Million BTUs of Total Energy
100 Pounds of Greenhouse Gases
545 Gallons of Wastewater
36 Pounds of Solid Waste

Left Coast Press, Inc. made this paper choice because our printer, Thomson-Shore, Inc., is a member of Green Press Initiative, a nonprofit program dedicated to supporting authors, publishers, and suppliers in their efforts to reduce their use of fiber obtained from endangered forests.

For more information, visit www.greenpressinitiative.org

Environmental impact estimates were made using the Environmental Defense Paper Calculator. For more information visit: www.papercalculator.org.